Evaluation of Library and Information Services

Second edition

John Crawford

INFORMATION MANAGEMENT

Is your organisation a corporate member of Aslib?

Aslib, The Association for Information Management, is a world class corporate membership organisation with over 2000 members in some 70 countries. Aslib actively promotes best practice in the management of information resources. It lobbies on all aspects of the management of, and legislation concerning, information at local, national and international levels.

Aslib provides consultancy and information services, professional development training, conferences, specialist recruitment, Internet products, and publishes primary and secondary journals, conference proceedings, directories and monographs.

Further information is available from:

Aslib, The Association for Information Management
Staple Hall
Stone House Court
London EC3A 7PB
Tel: +44 020 7903 0000
Fax: +44 020 7903 0011
Email: *aslib@aslib.com*
WWW: *http://www.aslib.com/*

Evaluation of Library and Information Services

Second edition

INFORMATION MANAGEMENT

Published by Aslib, The Association for Information Management and Information Management International
Staple Hall
Stone House Court
London EC3A 7PB
Tel: +44 020 7903 0000
Fax: +44 020 7903 0011
Email: *aslib@aslib.com*
WWW: *http://www.aslib.com*

ISBN 0 85142 443 0

Series Editor

Sylvia Webb is a well-known consultant, author and lecturer in the information management field. Her first book, *Creating an Information Service*, now in its third edition, was published by Aslib and has sold in over forty countries. She has experience of working in both the public and private sectors, ranging from public libraries to national and international organisations. She has also been a lecturer at Ashridge Management College, specialising in management and interpersonal skills, which led to her second book, *Personal Development in Information Work*, also published by Aslib. She has served on a number of government advisory bodies and is past Chair of the former Information and Library Services Lead Body, now the Information Services National Training Organisation which develops National Vocational Qualifications (NVQs) for the LIS profession. She is actively involved in professional education and training and is also a former Vice-President of the Institute of Information Scientists. As well as being editor of this series, Sylvia Webb has written three of the Know How Guides: *Making a charge for library and information services*, *Preparing a guide to your library and information service* and *Knowledge management: linchpin of change*.

A complete listing of all titles in the series can be found at the back of this volume.

About the author

John Crawford is Library Research Officer at Glasgow Caledonian University where he is responsible for the evaluation of library services and directing and conducting research projects. He holds degrees from the universities of London and Strathclyde and obtained his Ph.D. from Glasgow Caledonian University in 1994. He has written or co-authored some 40 articles, conference papers and contributions to books. His interests include the evaluation of library services, performance measurement, copyright, the library and information needs of non-traditional students and the historical aspects of librarianship. He is active in professional affairs and is chairman of the Library History Group.

Contents

Acknowledgements

For contributions to, or comments on text and information thanks to the following: Zoe Clarke and Peter Wynne at the Centre for Research in Library and Information Management (CERLIM), the participants at two workshops on performance measurement for the electronic library at the 4th European Serials Group conference in Manchester in April 1999, Guy Daines, Principal Policy Adviser at the Library Association, Stephen Town at RMCS Shrivenham, Barbara Stratton and colleagues at the Members' Information Centre at the Library Association, Toby Bainton at the Standing Conference of National and University Libraries (SCONUL), Kate Cole at Westminster Libraries & Archives, Carole Tucker at the Ministry of Defence HQ Information and Library Service, Lynda Clerk at the Scottish Agricultural Science Agency and Graham Bulpitt at Sheffield Hallam University. Thanks to Elizabeth for proof reading the text in draft.

I wish to acknowledge the following sources:

Glasgow Caledonian University for permission to reproduce the General Satisfaction Survey questionnaire; Don Revill and Geoffrey Ford for permission to reproduce the Poppleton Metropolitan University Library Services Survey (SCONUL), Jonathan Gordon for permission to reproduce the IPF public library questionnaire, Ann Saunders, Head of Community and Leisure, East Renfrewshire Council, for permission to reproduce a questionnaire and survey data and Sandra Mann, Library Manager at

The Open Polytechnic of New Zealand for permission to reproduce the Student Library Service Charter. And, not forgetting Willow, who, despite having achieved the status of a senior cat, still insists on having a paw in the writing up process.

Introduction, reasons for evaluation and related factors

Introduction

Whether we like it or not, we live in an evaluation culture. This is the result of social change over the past thirty years. The growth of the consumer movement in the 1970s encouraged consumers of goods and services to view much more critically the quality of service they received and to complain if they were not satisfied. From 1976 onwards declining patterns of public expenditure signalled the need to maximise resources and defend pre-existing patterns of expenditure, something which usually requires the collection of data. Declining public expenditure in the 80s was compounded by economic recession which encouraged consumers to spend more carefully and look critically at the goods and services they purchased.

Although librarians have been aware of the importance of meeting users' needs for decades, the customer care movement in the 90s has strengthened the emphasis on customer orientation. The movement originated in retailing, e.g. supermarkets, but has successfully transferred itself to the public sector. This new emphasis on the 'customer' has expressed itself in customer care statements and charters. The Citizens Charter in which a former

British Prime Minister was himself involved led, among other things, to the Library Association's model *Charter* which was produced at government prompting and which refers, inter alia, to the need for regular surveys. The effect has been less marked in higher education and special libraries. There are now higher education charters for both England and Scotland and some universities such as Liverpool John Moores have developed their own. It has a section on library provision.

The world in which all types of libraries function has come under the influence of a new world of analysis and assessment: the 'new managerialism' has promoted an emphasis on strategic planning, customer service and devolved budgeting in the public sector. Strategic planning has resulted in the introduction of mission statements and institutional targets/aims/goals etc. (Morgan 1995, p.14) and departments within the organisation, such as libraries, may have their own mission statements which can be used as a baseline for evaluation. Devolved budgeting and the need to identify costs to give the 'best value for money' carry with them an implication of evaluation. Compulsory competitive tendering in public libraries and market testing in government departments are good examples and can be linked to the emergence of quality departments in public libraries and the ideology of evaluation which is implied. More recently the British government has introduced a Best Value regime and is developing a Best Value Inspectorate under the control of the Audit Commission. All local authorities, including their library services, are involved. Fundamental Performance Reviews will take place in which 20% of library services will be evaluated every five years. There are four principles involved, the four Cs:

- Challenge
- Consult
- Compare
- Compete.

Local performance plans will be produced which will be updated annually according to centrally prescribed targets. Currently the Department for Culture, Media and Sport, the Library Association and the Local Government Association are circulating to local authorities and other interested parties, standards for consultation which will be used by the Best Value Inspectorate and the minister when evaluating the performance of individual authorities. They will also be used by the librarians of local authorities themselves in evaluating services and planning developments. The aim is to introduce a culture change into British local government and will lead to the appointment of Best Value Officers, essentially quality officers. It will certainly generate a regime of evaluation as yet unspecified.

In higher education the funding councils have created a regime of assessment under which specific subject areas are evaluated and library provision in the relevant subject area is reviewed as part of the Assessment. SCONUL (1997) has usefully produced an *Aide-memoire for assessors...* which conveniently lists the main relevant issues. However this is not a holistic process and libraries are only reviewed in the context of their contribution to individual programmes. For example, in 1997-98 the Scottish Higher Education Funding Council (1998) reviewed 11 subject areas and commented on library facilities. These are generally positive although there are the usual comments about pressure on resources including declining book budgets and restricted opening hours. Comments on staff were generally favourable and there was a noticeable emphasis on IT and electronic information services. In some cases specific academic libraries have submitted themselves to evaluation in the same manner as teaching departments. The library services review at the University of Northumbria in 1996-97 is a good example (Willoughby 1999). This was occasioned by a need to restructure and reduce staff costs. Among the anticipated needs were: a major shift to a self-service culture; a concentration of service delivery into periods of greatest use and an increase in electronic service delivery. After an extensive period of data collection and opinion gathering outcomes included improvements in reshelving, more rapid development of electronic services, a centralised and enlarged short loan collection and a gradual move to self-service provision. Enquiry services were reduced and opening hours adjusted to meet patterns of use. Survey work was essential, both during the review and in evaluating the changes which had been made.

In special libraries the quality management programmes of parent organisations have affected the library. The formalised quality initiatives: Investors in people, Charter Mark and BS/EN/ISO9000 (formerly ISO/BS5750 in the UK) have been applied mainly in public libraries but only by about a quarter surveyed at the time. BS/EN/ISO9000 is the least popular (Usherwood 1995. p.272). Charter Mark recipients include Kent County Arts & Library service and the library services of the London boroughs of Bromley and Croydon (Brophy & Coulling 1996. p.65). The Charter Mark award, administered by the Cabinet Office, continues to attract applicants of whom 365 were successful in 1997 (Cabinet Office 1998). A further 151 which came close to meeting the judges' requirements received a certificate of commendation. To discourage complacency the award lasts for only three years and can be withdrawn during the period of the award. The judges require applicants to:

- Set clear, tough and meaningful performance standards.
- Tell users in a clear, straightforward way about services.
- Consult widely about what services people need and how services can be improved.
- Make services available to everyone who needs them.
- Treat all people fairly. Have polite and helpful staff.
- Make it easy for people to say when they are not happy with the service.
- Use resources effectively by budgeting carefully.
- Continually make improvements.
- Work with other providers to provide a better service.

•   And you need to show that your users agree
      that you provide a really good service.

An example of a library which has won the Charter Mark award is the Health Promotion Library
Scotland (HPLS) which is one of only 31 services
in Scotland to receive a Charter Mark. HPLS is the
library at the Health Education Board for Scotland
(Hebs). It is a national information resource and
holds Scotland's most comprehensive collection of
books, reports and journals on health promotion
and health education. The library staff decided to
apply for a Charter Mark because although they
felt they provided a good service there was room
for improvement and they wanted to offer something even better. The Charter Mark scheme was
chosen because of its unique focus on the service
the customer receives. The staff believed it would
enable them to improve their service and give them
recognition for what they were already doing. Although senior staff took the lead in the application
all staff were encouraged to be innovative and im-
aginative in coming up with ideas to improve the
service and obtain good user feedback. Initiatives
which arose as a direct consequence of the application included extra training in customer care and
disability awareness, improved suggestions and
complaints procedures, baby-changing facilities,
regular user surveys, a user panel and a user service policy and standards which are advertised and
regularly measured. The most significant source of
help, however, proved to be the actual assessment
and the detailed feedback report which provided
suggestions on how to improve further. The successful application helped the library in perform-

ance standards and measurement, customer care, value for money, user satisfaction and planning improvements. It also helped in team building (Forrest & Mackay 1999).

Linked with pressures from the outside there have been changes within libraries. New services have been introduced. In some libraries opening hours have been extended or altered to meet new patterns of usage. Public libraries provide services targeted at ethnic minorities and other special groups. Since the early 80s electronic services have been making an impact, initially in the form of automated library systems with OPACs. These were followed by CD-ROMs and more recently web-based networked services such as EDINA and R & D programmes such as *elib* which has involved, *inter alia*, the digitisation of books and journal articles. More recently it has supported 'hybrid' programmes like Hylife and Headline which have been notable for their needs analysis and evaluation components. These new developments in turn generate a need to evaluate these new services to test their effectiveness and justify the money spent on them. Automated library systems, although they produce management information data, have on the whole produced data for only a small number of performance indicators (Clarke, McDougall & Fisher 1998 pp. 405-412).

As services have become more sophisticated so their users have been increasingly vocal in commenting on them and criticising them. This has been greatly facilitated by the growth of formal mechanisms for comment and complaint: universities have programme boards with student representatives who comment on and, if necessary, complain about the quality of the education they receive. This can include reports upon library services. Staff/student committees and library committees fulfil the same function. In public libraries the *Which* report of February 1990 showed that public libraries could be evaluated in high profile consumer journals, just like any other service, and commercial surveying bodies like MORI have done work on public library services. Complainers, formerly regarded as a nuisance are now seen more as an asset (*Independent: Business review* 12.5.1999. p.2). Regular customers expect a better service and rising complaints mean that they are prepared to expend the energy to achieve it. A complaint is therefore seen as a gift that a customer gives to a business to help it perform better.

The changing nature of library management itself has generated a need for evaluation and enhanced the possibilities of analysis. Automation has reduced the need for staffing in technical services operations and sometimes in counter staffing. While this makes it possible to redeploy staff to the 'front of the house' the impact on the service users receive needs to be evaluated. The internet has spawned 'learning centres' in different types of libraries whose use needs evaluation and a new type of user, 'the lifelong learner', whose study and IT skills may well have been overestimated by the UK government.

In the mid 1990s a number of influential reports appeared which affected developments. These included: *Review of the public library service in England and Wales for the Department of National Heritage: final report* (London: Aslib, 1995), which, interestingly enough, recommended 'a move away from ... mechanistic standards with an emphasis on population, area and quantity and towards the creation of active, service-centred standards developed through a people and provider partnership'; Joint Funding Councils' Libraries Review Group *Report* (Bristol: Higher EducationFunding Council for England (Follett Report), 1993) is a collection of statistics and review of services which promoted the 'electronic library' in higher education. The *Report* spawned the Electronic Libraries Programme which has provided funding for R & D work in academic libraries and has fostered a research and evaluation culture among academic librarians; Joint Funding Councils *The effective academic library: a framework for evaluating the performance of UK academic libraries* (Bristol: Higher Education Funding Council for England, 1995) is another offspring of Follett and offered a 'basket' of measures for performance measurement.

Clearly a culture of evaluation exists in libraries and there are many potential areas for development. However there is a need to develop a core of concerns and methodologies which is the aim of this book.

Reasons for evaluation

There are differing ideas about what evaluation is and why it should be done. Blagden (1990, pp. 4-23) provides a useful summary. The management approach sees monitoring performance as an integral part of good management which is undertaken for two reasons:

1) to convince the funders and the clients that the service is delivering the benefits that were expected when the investment was made

2) as an internal control mechanism to ensure that the resources are used efficiently and effectively.

This approach has been informed by a decade of cost cutting. Another approach is to look at cost benefit analysis and value of the service while a third is to view the library as a set of systems. Bawden (1990) explains the importance of evaluation and discusses various methodologies, including user-orientated evaluation which aims to improve services and the competence and motivation of librarians. This signals a move towards evaluation from the viewpoint of the users, which has been the hallmark of the 90s.

It is important to distinguish between evaluation and performance measurement. According to Abbott (1994, p.2,9) "Performance indicators are simply management tools designed to assist library managers to determine how well their service is performing. They provide evidence on which to base judgements, but are not substitutes for that judgement, since performance data needs to be interpreted before such assessments can be made. In considering performance indicators we are rarely dealing with absolutes'.

Performance indicators contribute to the process of evaluation but the latter is a broader term for the assessment of performance. As indicated above there are different approaches to assessment. Lancaster (1993) advocates approaching evaluation from the perspective of performance measurement and uses a systematic approach. It is a method which emphasises technical services issues, e.g. weeding of stock, and illustrates a tension between the two main types of measure: technical services and user-orientated measures. The former have a strong quantitative emphasis and may impact on services to users e.g. speed of cataloguing sought materials, while user orientated measures are more qualitative and might well be those which users would choose themselves.

The primary focus of this book is the evaluation of services provided to the user: how they may be identified, how a background understanding of them may be built up, how they can be evaluated and how the data collected can be put to good use. Superficially, librarianship is easily evaluated because it is mainly about the provision of discrete, related and comprehensive services which have an element of predictability about their operation. However, services with a major qualitative component such as reference services are difficult to evaluate and the methods used may be controversial. The volume of activity in a service has to be related to the demand for it to understand if it functions well. The service must be appropriate to the need of the user which, in turn raises the question: What is a user? Are users an amorphous mass with identical needs or are they discrete groups with differing or even contradictory needs? Although progress has been made in evaluation of services to users there is still a need for simple, generally agreed definitions: What is a queue? What does answering the telephone promptly mean? Fortunately thanks to such documents as the *Effective academic library,* the LA *Charter* and ISO 11620 (see p. 27) such definitions are beginning to emerge and the growth of the quality movement encourages us to think in terms of heterogeneous groups of users and customer satisfaction (Brophy & Coulling 1996. pp. 39-52).

Specific issues in evaluation

There are many reasons for undertaking evaluation but the main ones are listed below.

1. The principal and overriding reason for the evaluation of library services is to collect information to facilitate decision-making and justify increasing expenditure or defending existing expenditure.

2. To evaluate the quality of service provided: both overall, and specifically to plan for future improvements. This is usually done by surveying, either quantitative or qualitative, and there may be operational difficulties, some specified under objectives 3-8.

3. To identify the extent to which problems can be solved. It may or may not be possible to solve a problem identified by evaluation. If a problem identified by evaluation cannot be solved this is usually due to:

a)   resource constraints e.g. a survey by a public
       library may indicate the need to employ an
       ethnic minorities librarian but budgetary con-
       straints may delay or make this impossible.
       In this case, at least, evaluation can contrib-
       ute to the planning process.

b)   The involvement of parties outside the li-
       brary's control e.g. evaluation of a university
       library's exam paper collection may indicate
       considerable user dissatisfaction because of
       its incompleteness, which, in turn, is due to
       the University administration's failure to sup-
       ply the Library with complete sets of papers.
       This leaves the library with several choices,
       ranging from doing nothing to undertaking
       new work.

4. To identify differing or contradictory needs of
different user categories. It is a serious error to as-
sume that all library users have the same needs and
that to benefit one group is to benefit all. For example, short loan collections in academic libraries benefit full-time students disproproportionately
because full-time students always 'get there first'.
Part-time and distance learners find such a service
less suited to their needs because of their irregular
contact with the campus.

5. To plan public relations work and information
dissemination. Evaluation may point to user ignorance in particular areas e.g. the photocopying service provided and the photocopying regulations
imposed by the 1988 Copyright Act. This may in-
dicate a need for an appropriate leaflet. Similarly
ignorance about the use of electronic information

services might suggest changes in user education in an academic library.

6. To provide feedback to, and to evaluate contractors e.g. time taken by booksellers to supply items, and quality of OPACs. Such measures impinge on the technical services approach but have important implications for users. An OPAC with poor functionality or user-friendliness may only be modifiable in conjunction with the system supplier. A clear identification of user difficulties can strengthen the library's hand in negotiating with systems suppliers.

7. To involve users in management. A consequence of the rise of the profession of librarianship in the 20th century has been the exclusion of users from library management, where, in the case of publicly available libraries, and to a lesser extent, academic libraries, they were once pre-eminent. Regular evaluation of services, by whatever means, allows users to rediscover a voice in library management and express views about service priorities.

8. To provide the basis of further improvements and direction. It may be that evaluation will merely highlight the library's ignorance of a particular issue and the need for further work. This is particularly the case in brief overview surveys which often point to issues like quality of stock and the need to improve the situation.

9. Closing the feedback loop. Recent research in higher education has shown that it essential to report to users on the outcomes of survey work and the decisions taken as a result. This shows the user

that evaluation is a valid exercise to which they have contributed. Failure to close the feedback loop may be the reason for the phenomenon known as 'questionnaire fatigue'.

1. Identifying Performance Issues for Evaluation

It is important to devise a systematic regime of assessment which meets the needs of the library and can be understood outside the library by a parent body or users. This usually involves an annual overview survey to identify more general problems, backed up by a range of methods, to clarify specific issues. It helps to know where you 'fit in'. John Sumsion, former head of the Library and Information Statistics Unit has devised a classification of universities as follows (Sumsion 1994):

1) large and postgraduate and miscellaneous

2) pre-1960 universities

3) post-1960 pre-1992 universities

4) 1992 universities (former polytechnics)

5) HE colleges: education and general

6) HE specialist colleges.

This gives a basic guide to comparative perspectives and the kind of issue a particular academic library should concern itself with. Floor space for large special collections is unlikely to be a major issue in a post-1992 academic library. Public library service points can also be categorised as 'large' or 'medium', depending on the range and level of services they provide. Opening hours per week can be used as a basis for categorisation (Library Association 1995).

Before beginning to look into the question of what to evaluate it is worth asking: Is a survey really necessary? Can adequate data be obtained from pre-existing sources which might supply you with a comparative perspective and eliminate the need for further work? Some sources are listed below but the Library and Information Statistics Unit at Loughborough University has now emerged as the key provider and indeed interpreter of LIS statistics in the UK and their website is often a good place to start.

Sources to inform the identification of evaluation issues include the following:

Internal/local sources

1. Mission statements, whether of the library or the parent body, will list objectives which might be fairly specific. A University mission statement, for example, might include a declaration that it wishes to have a wide range of modes of attendance so that it can recruit students who would find it difficult to attend on a normal full-time basis. Such students might have difficulty in making the best use of the library's services and a study of their needs could be undertaken.

2. Course/programme board reports. Specific university courses are managed by course or programme boards which include student and library representatives. They give both staff and students a forum for comment and complaint about central

services. In addition, annual reports are usually produced in which students can comment on library services. In practice these tend to be repetitive and focus on a limited number of issues like availability of basic textbooks, access to seating, noise and loan regulations. Nevertheless they represent a useful forum of undergraduate opinion, and taken in conjunction with other sources, can help to identify problems requiring further attention, even if they are the most intractable.

3. Library committees and published sources. Most types of library have a library committee. In public libraries it has a statutory function. In academic and special libraries its role varies from decision making body to a talking shop. Much will depend on whether the members bring issues to it or whether business is led by library staff, in which case it is less likely to produce potential evaluation issues. A supplementary and much more anarchic source is contributions to newspapers and inhouse journals. Letters to local newspapers can stimulate debate on public library issues and in universities student newspapers are a popular platform for debate and complaint. Unfortunately, although frequently impassioned, such sources are not always as thoughtful and well-informed as they might be.

4. Institutional programmes of evaluation which evaluate all the services provided by the parent institution, on a regular basis, are still relatively uncommon. Such an approach is useful because it compares the Library with other services and gives an idea of its status within the institution as a whole. Institutional programmes of evaluation,

apart from the obvious purposes of informing decision-making and identifying issues for further study, can be used as a basis for charter design as they give a picture of the level of service which can realistically be provided in specific areas.

5. Management information sources can offer a starting point for evaluation. The advent of automated systems has eliminated the need to do basic survey work. It should be easy to extract information from automated systems about particular categories of user and the use they make of loan and inter-library-loan services. Simple usage statistics can be the start of an investigation into the worth of specific services.

6. Most types of library have a structure of meetings, from a simple staff meeting in small libraries to a complex system of team and related meetings in large libraries. Sometimes this is supplemented by 'limited life' working parties. Such meetings will discuss issues specific to themselves or matters of general concern. Problems they raise may be the subject of evaluation.

7. Electronic bulletin boards and suggestions boxes offer users an opportunity to express themselves directly to users. The specific advantages and disadvantages of this are discussed in Chapter 3. In general terms they allow users to raise qualitative issues which, if they occur sufficiently frequently can identify problems which need further study.

8. Programmes of research to identify evaluation issues: if resources permit it is worthwhile considering a programme of research to identify what the

library's ongoing performance issues are likely to be and to try to devise a systematic programme of evaluation. As indicated above, there are different theories as to what constitutes evaluation and many libraries identify a programme of basic needs and an *ad hoc* programme of supplementary evaluation which looks at specific issues. An overall 'holistic' programme of evaluation is therefore lacking. The major disadvantage of this approach is its proneness to inflexibility and, in a period of rapid change, the performance issues identified can become out of date.

Published sources

General

Blagden, J & Harrington, J (1990) *How good is your library? : a review of approaches to the evaluation of library and information services.* London: Aslib. Although now somewhat out-of-date this is still a good starting point for research. It is divided into two sections. The first section identifies survey issues and the different approaches to what constitutes evaluation. The advantages and disadvantages of various methodologies are considered. There is a useful discussion on the controversial issue of unobtrusive testing. The second section comprises an annotated bibliography.

Creaser, C & Murphy, A (1999) *LISU annual library statistics 1999: featuring trend analysis of UK public and academic libraries 1988-98. Including Public Library Statistics Report No. 13* Loughborough: LISU. Statistically speaking, the best place to start. It summarises key statistics for a wide range of library and information work in the UK. The data is for 1997-98 and where possible trend analyses for the past ten years are included. About half the text is devoted to public libraries. The university libraries section has analyses for old and new universities. There is data on national libraries and a section on school and special libraries. There is also a useful bibliography.

Public libraries

King Research Ltd. (1990) *Keys to success: performance indicators for public libraries.* (Library Information series no. 18). London: Office of Arts and Libraries. This was the first successful manual of performance indicators for public libraries and was published with the intention of encouraging public librarians to use quantitative methods of setting and assessing performance standards. It lists 21 performance measures and 16 performance indicators with explanations as to how they are applied. There is also a useful section on survey techniques and statistical measures. Very much a practical reference manual.

Sumsion, J (1993) *Practical performance indicators – 1992. Documenting the Citizen's Charter consultation for UK public libraries with examples of PIs and surveys in use. (Occasional Paper no. 5).* Loughborough: LISU. It links library evaluation with the Citizens' Charter and gives practical examples of surveys and performance indicators. It lists performance indicators proposed to the Audit Commission in two categories: mandatory and 'voluntary' with a summary of outcomes. Appendices include examples of statistical data, performance indicators and questionnaires, followed by examples of studies done by particular authorities. These are good examples for practitioners and suggest how data can be presented as well as collected.

Review of the public library service in England and Wales for the Department of National Heritage: final report. (1995) London: Aslib. At the time of its publication this aimed to be a landmark report on public libraries. Although somewhat out-of-date it is still useful. It contains information about charters and standards, a wide range of statistical materials, information about funding and a discussion about changes in the service. Examples of surveys are included in an appendix.

Audit Commission (1997) *Due for renewal: a report on the library service.* London: Audit Commission. Deals with 'value for money' aspects of service quality: better planning, costing by service function, partnerships including partnerships with other local authority departments, better stock management and grasping the opportunities offered by information and communication technologies.

Department of National Heritage (1997) *Reading the future: a review of public libraries in England.* London: Department for Culture, Media and Sport. Stipulates the need for library plans, benchmarking of important performance areas and a list of key performance indicators. The performance indicators are likely to become (with some minor amendments) the ones for which information is required from public libraries over the next few years.

CIPFA (1999) *Public library statistics 1998/99 actuals.* London: CIPFA. Gives comparative data on which to base one's own performance. Covers the whole of the British Isles, usually including the Republic of Ireland. It includes the questionnaire on which returns are based. Now in its 38th year.

Bohme S & Spiller, D (1999) *Perspectives of public library use 2: a compendium of survey information.* Loughborough: LISU. An up-to-date survey and a good place for the beginner to start. It is a compendium of statistical data collected by LISU and the Book Marketing Council, supplemented by recent LISU research and work by local authorities. This last feature is particularly useful as it illustrates the kind of research which practitioners have found useful. It is divided into eight sections which include key public library statistics; extracts and survey summaries from various sources which examine aspects of the public library service at a national level, including the CIPFA Plus user satisfaction survey findings for 1997; summaries of user surveys including studies of children using the library and one of Asian users; research on information and communications technology and the results of a variety of surveys on information and reference services. There is also a compendium of book trade statistics.

College libraries

Library Association. Colleges of Further and Higher Education Group (1995) *Guidelines for college libraries: recommendations for performance and resourcing* 5th ed. London: Library Association Publishing.

Has a section on quality assurance listing essential client satisfaction and key performance indicators for college libraries.

Scottish Library & Information Council & Scottish Library Association (1997) *Libraries in Scottish further education colleges: standards for performance and resourcing*. Motherwell: Scottish Library & Information Council. Includes a list of performance indicators and a 'Self-Evaluation Quality Framework'.

HEFC Colleges Learning Resources Group (1999) *Statistics 1997/98*. HCLRG. This statistical series, inspired by the SCONUL statistics, is now in its fifth year. Reflects the diversity and size of libraries in this sector, so overview figures derived from it have to be applied with care. Now includes 53 libraries, mostly in England.

University libraries

Van House, N, Weil, BT & McClure, C R (1990) *Measuring academic library performance: a practical approach*. Chicago: American Library Association. Contains examples of surveys in specific areas, examples of questionnaires which can be photocopied and guidance in their administration and analysis. Although now somewhat old it influenced the former COPOL and also SCONUL which has based questionnaires on it.

Joint Funding Councils' Libraries Review Group (1993) *Report*. Bristol: Higher Education Funding Council for England. (Follett Report). Both useful in itself as a contemporary survey and for the other initiatives which it spawned. It includes a proposed framework of performance indicators and draws attention to the need for qualitative, as well as quantitative measures, although this is not developed in detail.

Joint Funding Councils (1995) *The effective academic library: a framework for evaluating the performance of UK academic libraries.* Bristol: Higher Education Funding Council for England. Provides a 'basket' of five groups of indicators: integration, user satisfaction, delivery, efficiency and economy. While it avoids details and uses clear terminology, it reflects a traditional approach and does not give sufficient emphasis to converged services or electronically based sources of information. It does not reflect the work of research libraries and some indicators considered optional, e.g. speed of reshelving, would be considered by many to be fundamental.

Barton, J & and Blagden, J (1998) *Academic library effectiveness: a comparative approach.* London: British Library Research and Innovation Centre. (British Library Research and Innovation Report 120). Building on *The effective academic library* the report has developed a small set of management statistics to be used by funding bodies. It also discusses key performance issues and makes some suggestions for the future.

SCONUL (1999) *Annual library statistics 1997-98.* London: SCONUL: The main statistical series for university libraries. It lists a wide range of statistics for 112 returns out of a possible 124 institutions, a response rate of 90%. Each section concludes with a mean against which the figures for an individual library may be compared.

SCONUL Newsletter. Useful for short reports on local evaluation activities

Special libraries

Creaser, C & Spiller, D (1997) *TFPL survey of UK special library statistics.* Loughborough: LISU. (LISU Occasional Paper no. 15). A step towards the evaluation of an under-reported area. Includes sections on management and users, staff, funding, electronic services, printed materials and other stock, other services and automation. There is a trend analysis and a summary of results by sector.

Spiller, D, Creaser, C & Murphy, A. (1998) *Libraries in the workplace.* Loughborough: LISU. (LISU Occasional Paper no. 20). Aims to provide an overview of key issues and trends in 'libraries in the workplace' i.e. government, business and the professions. Surveys ten library 'sectors' including government departments, commercial and financial companies and pharmaceutical companies. It is intended to lead to annual data collection and trend analysis.

School and children's libraries

Library Association (1997) Survey *of UK secondary school libraries 1997.* London: Library Association. Executive summary only. Full report available on the Library Association's Web page: http://www.la-hq.org.uk/ssl97.htm. The first UK survey of secondary school libraries. Covers *inter alia* bookstock and other resources, borrowing, staffing, spending, curriculum development and ICT.

Creaser, C & and Murphy, A (1999) *A survey of library services to schools and children in the UK 1998-99*. Loughborough: LISU. The tenth report in this series which has included Scotland and Northern Ireland since 1991-92. Includes a trend analysis over the last five years in a number of key measures for both schools library services and public library services to children.

Spreadbury, H & Spiller, D. (1999) *Survey of secondary school library users*, Loughborough: LISU. (LISU Occasional Paper no. 21). A report of a survey of about 400 pupils, aged 11 to 18 at four London schools. This revealed striking differences in library use between different age groups and between state and independent schools. The questionnaire used is included.

Performance indicator manuals

It is worth being aware of these because they prescribe definitions and reliable survey methodologies for applying particular indicators which can be directly used in internal survey work and the use of standardised methodologies makes comparisons with other institutions possible.

Poll, R & te Boekhorst, P (1996) *Measuring quality: international guidelines for performance measurement in academic libraries*. Munchen: Saur (IFLA Publications 76). Lists 17 indicators which can be applied to academic libraries worldwide. Each indicator is accompanied by suggested methodologies which can be used in survey work.

British Standards Institution (1998) *Information and documentation: library performance indicators.* London: BSI. (International Standard ISO 11620). This International Standard is applicable to all types of libraries in all countries. It includes 25 definitions of standard terms used with performance indicators and the criteria which a performance indicator should meet. The indicators included are either in widespread use or well documented in the literature and are seen to be most useful for libraries in general. Some 29 indicators are described which cover mainstream activities such as user perception, providing, retrieving and lending documents and enquiry and reference services. Detailed methodologies are given for applying each indicator and these can be used in planning and implementing survey work.

In conclusion it is worthwhile mentioning electronic discussion lists as a useful source of information. Lis-link is particularly useful and simple surveys are often undertaken and reported via it. It is most useful to academic and special librarians. There are two specialised lists: lis-qual and lis-perf-measures. All are currently accessed via Mailbase at http://www.mailbase.ac.uk/

2. Quantitative methods

Questionnaires: for and against

Survey work, in whatever form, is the most widely used method of evaluating library services and the questionnaire is widely viewed as the most attractive method of quantitative data collection. It can be applied to a whole range of issues from a simple overview survey of user satisfaction to a detailed investigation of the needs of small groups of users. However the structure of the questionnaire and its method of administration will vary, depending on the user group being addressed.

To its exponents, the quantitative, questionnaire-based approach has distinct advantages. The questionnaire can report on the views of many thousands of people and give a breadth of data not available to qualitative methods. It adopts a highly structured approach and because it uses statistical methods and produces numerical data its outcomes are perceived to be 'scientific' and therefore objectively correct. If well-designed, it gives clear-cut answers to the questions asked and because interested parties can complete it without intervention it appears to be neutral. It is good for asking questions based on counts: 'How often do you visit the library?' A questionnaire offering a limited number of answer options of the YES/NO or tick box variety (closed questions) can be analysed relatively easily and quickly.

However, as a method, it has the vices of its virtues. Because it is highly structured it is also highly inflexible. If a fault is found in a questionnaire halfway through its administration, not much can be done about it. It does not penetrate the attitudes which inform the answers. A questionnaire might readily reveal that Saturday opening does not appeal to part-time students, although superficially Saturday opening might seem attractive to people who work during the week. Behind the answer lies the complex world of the part-time student who has to juggle family, social, occupational and study commitments. Furthermore the questionnaire answers only the questions which have been asked. If important issues have not been addressed by the questionnaire then its qualitative value will be diminished. At its worst extreme it is possible to design a questionnaire which, by selecting questions which focus on certain issues and avoiding others, could produce a misleading result. For example it might be possible to get an over-favourable view of a library service by avoiding asking questions about service areas which users consider to be poor. While such goings-on are unknown in librarianship it is interesting to note that precisely such a charge has been made against Britain's privatised railway companies (*Independent* 7.1.1999). The accurate identification of the performance issues which inform question selection is at the heart of good questionnaire design. Finally, although the analysis of a questionnaire should produce useful generalisations it is not the outcome of a collective experience. Questionnaires are completed by individuals and represent the views of individuals. They are not a group experience.

Some issues for study

There are a wide range of issues suitable for study. Here are a few examples:

1) An overview user or general satisfaction survey which aims to produce a general picture of user satisfaction. This is used in all types of library. It often identifies issues for further study but its main purpose is to effect service improvements.

2) Materials availability survey which tries to establish whether users found the books, journals or other sources they were looking for, usually on a particular day.

3) A reference satisfaction survey which invites the user to evaluate the quality of the reference service received. Again this usually relates to a particular day or otherwise limited time period.

4) Benchmarking – a comparison of one library's performance with many others. This presupposes the existence of a comparative database of edited data.

5) Ethnic origin: mainly used by public libraries to understand library use by ethnic minorities.

6) Lapsed users surveys – used mainly by public libraries to estimate the library services' penetration into the community.

7) Opening hours: to plan the extension or alteration of opening hours.

The availability of data from automated systems reduces the need for data collection in areas which have a systemic element. Some aspects of satisfaction with an inter-library-loans service can be inferred from statistics and benchmarking with other institutions but there might still be a need to collect the views of users who attach a lot of importance to the service, like research fellows and research students in higher education. Problems like length of queues can be tackled by simple counts and may not need to involve the user at all. In public libraries some survey priorities are: impact, market penetration, promotion of services, book buying compared with borrowing, information/enquiry services, audio-visual services and electronic information sources (Spiller 1998, p. 77).

Questionnaire design

In questionnaire design standardised methodologies should be used as much as possible. The sources referred to Chapter 1 will help. Volumes like Van House et al (1990) and the IPF manual (1995) are particularly useful. Standardised methodologies allow you to benefit from the experience of others and to compare your results with similar libraries.

Although some questionnaires use an A3 format e.g. the IPF National Standard User Survey offers this as an option, the A4 format is widespread and influences the design and structure of the questionnaire. The Committee of Vice-Chancellors and Principals of the Universities of the United Kingdom (1993 pp. 29-52) recommends short questionnaires and quotes examples of questionnaires occupying only one side of A4 . The one sheet of A4 format is ideal for a short user survey but less attractive for longer questionnaires where several sheets might be necessary to avoid crowding. Unfortunately long questionnaires can be off-putting and are perhaps best reserved for small populations with a high level of commitment to the library or the survey. Special library users and research students are obvious examples.

In general questionnaire questions should proceed from the general to the specific. General questions which do not intimidate the respondent will encourage progression to more specific ones. If questionnaires are broken up into components or 'question modules' within each module again progression should be from general to specific. It is a good idea to leave a fair amount of white space on the paper so that the respondent does not feel overwhelmed by a mass of print.

There are essentially two types of question: closed (or precoded) and open (free response) questions. In closed questions the respondent is offered a choice of answers and ticks or circles the most appropriate one. In open questions respondents can answer spontaneously in their own words. (Morgan 1995, 142-143.) The closed question is much easier to analyse, especially by computer, but it is essential that the options offered should be appropriate to the respondent. Here it is essential to build on the experience of others and carefully identify in advance the performance issues which will inform the design of your questionnaire questions. The answers to open questions can be much more instructive and entertaining to read but the comments made have to be turned into identifiable performance issues which can then be quantified. This is a time-consuming and somewhat subjective exercise. However the points made contribute to the identification of performance issues and therefore to modifications to the questionnaire in the future.

Specific points in questionnaire design

1) Don't ask a question unless you need to know the answer. Always be guided by the general aim of your survey and avoid peripheral or extraneous questions. They will only bulk out the questionnaire and make it less attractive to respondents. It will also lengthen analysis time.

2) Ask only questions which can be answered. This may seem so obvious as not to require stating, but questions should be avoided which require respondents to undertake significant data collection themselves.

3) Ask only questions which can be realistically and truthfully answered. Don't encourage the respondent to give speculative or inaccurate information. This applies particularly to open questions.

4) Ask only questions which the user is prepared to answer. Avoid questions which the respondent might consider embarrassing. Put sensitive questions (e.g. sex, age) last.

5) Ask only for information unavailable by other means. As indicated in Chapter 1 a great deal of survey and statistical data exists in published sources. Don't re-invent the wheel.

6) Ask precise rather than general questions. Avoid questions like. 'Are you satisfied/dissatisfied with the library service'. They are insufficiently probing and likely to mask dissatisfaction with specific areas of the service.

7) Avoid double questions like 'Would you like more books and a longer loan period'. They are different issues and should be treated separately. To put them together will lead to confused analysis.

8) Use simple jargon-free language. Questions should be short, simple and easy to grasp. Jargon is a particular problem in a jargon-filled profession like librarianship and can be difficult to avoid. I once designed an OPAC satisfaction survey questionnaire in conjunction with a Psychology student and a university lecturer, expert in questionnaire design. Despite this, respondents criticised what they perceived as jargon in the terminology of the questions. Jargon is very difficult to avoid in a survey which focuses on users' perceptions of technical issues. In libraries with a privileged user group, in frequent contact with the service, jargon may be more acceptable.

9) Avoid 'gift' questions such as 'Would you like Sunday opening?'. The respondent is unlikely to say 'no' even if he or she does not intend to make use of such a service himself or herself. It is better,

although more long-winded to offer a range of viable options e.g.

> 'The Library is considering opening on Sundays. If this were to be done would you prefer:
>
> • 11.00am to 4pm
> • 09.00am to 1pm
> • 1pm to 5pm
>
> Circle one'

The question is indicating to the respondent what the library can reasonably deliver and is inviting him or her to make a responsible choice.

10) Appreciate that the respondent may perceive a hidden agenda in the question. A survey of a service which is not widely used but valued by those who do use it may be interpreted by users as a signal that it will be withdrawn. This may result in misleading answers. Surveys of the use of infrequently used periodicals are a good example.

Sampling

Sampling is done when it is not possible to survey an entire population. This procedure is known as collecting *inferential statistics* which try to make statements about the parent population from the evidence of the sample. This is typically done when surveying public library users or university undergraduates. In the case of a small group of users it is possible to survey the entire population (doing a census). This usually applies to special libraries or small groups of users with specific needs e.g. the disabled. Samples aim to represent the population on a small scale and if the sample is reliable it should be possible to reach conclusions about the whole population.

The term *sampling frame* means a list of the entire population as defined by whatever factors are applied, such as gender or occupation. It may be a register of borrowers, university student records or a list of staff who work for a company and use a special library. Sampling theory demands that probability should be allowed to operate fully and therefore samples should be chosen randomly. There are a number of methods of random sampling:

1) Simple random sampling: each member of the (sampling frame) population has an equal chance of being chosen. If not many people are involved their names can be written on a piece of paper and drawn from a hat. Where many people are involved a table of random numbers can be used.

2) Systematic random sampling: this also involves the use of a sampling frame. A starting point is selected at random and then every *n*th number thereafter, fourth, tenth or whatever, depending on the size of the sample desired.

3) Stratified random sampling: the sampling frame is divided by criteria like library users by department or faculty, and random sampling takes place within each band chosen.

> To stratify you have to know that each group is different. This is difficult to do accurately and it might be useful to use proportionate sampling to ensure that the numbers for each band reflect the numbers in the sampling frame.

It is not always possible for a library to carry out a structured survey and there are also non-random and therefore less reliable methods which are widely used:

1) Accidental sampling: whoever is available is chosen.

2) Quota sampling: Whoever is available is chosen on the basis of predetermined characteristics such as age, gender, social class and occupation and a certain number of people have to be surveyed in each category. It is a quick method and convenient to administer and is widely used for opinion polling.

3) Purposive sampling: the survey population is chosen from prior knowledge, using intuition and judgement.

The relative validity of these methods depends on the purpose of the survey. Non-random methods can give more information about minority views. Random methods, by their very nature, are unlikely to generate many respondents from minority interest groups. This is the case in higher education where the views of the largest single group, full-time undergraduates will predominate, unless the views of other groups are sought as well. Quota sampling is a good method of surveying changes of opinion over time. The survey would have to be repeated at intervals to build up a meaningful, long term picture.

Practical advice on sample sizes

Although samples must be a certain minimum size (a rule of thumb might be 30) accuracy and representativeness are important in determining sample size. The bigger the sample the longer it will take to analyse the resulting data and the higher the administrative costs will be. Van House et al (1990, p.28) recommend 400 survey forms returned for their General Satisfaction Survey. Considerably fewer are permissible for the Reference Satisfaction Survey and Online Search Evaluation. Priority Search Ltd (PSL) of Sheffield which produces survey software for academic libraries specifies a minimum of 500 correctly completed questionnaires. SCONUL (1996) offers advice on sample sizes and desirable response rates for its five standard questionnaires. For the General Satisfaction Survey a response rate of 55-60% should be expected and a minimum of 400 responses is necessary for comprehensive analysis. For public libraries the IPF manual recommends sample sizes of between 740 and 1060, depending on the size of authority. It also suggests adding another 30% to these sample sizes to cater for non-response. An American body, the National Educational Association, has produced a formula, from which a table has been devised, giving recommended sample sizes for populations, ranging from 10 to 1,000,000 (Krejcie & Morgan 1970). Sample size calculators can be found on the World Wide Web. An example is http:/

/www.group-iv.com/resources/calculator.html
where by entering, for example, a population size
of 15,000 a required sample size of 375 is given.

Questionnaire administration

Before administering a questionnaire it is advisable
to pilot it. This helps to eliminate errors before the
questionnaire is actually administered. Problems
likely to be encountered include poor choice of terminology and varying interpretations of the questions due to ambiguous or misleading wording or
simply, the differing viewpoints of respondents. Ideally the pilot should be tried out on 10% of the intended sample. This can, in itself, be quite a large
number and it might not be possible, in which case
at least some of the sample should be consulted. It
is also a good idea to seek the advice of experts.
Universities, business and industry and local authorities usually employ people skilled in survey or
market research techniques, and they will often
offer advice or even direct help in planning and
organising survey work.

In administering questionnaires a range of practical, tactical and even ethical issues must be considered. It is not thought appropriate, in the United
Kingdom, to survey minors so persons under the
age of 16 cannot be asked to complete questionnaires. Information can be elicited from children
by interviewing and this is best done with a par-
ent/guardian or teacher present. It is also advisable to find out if any other survey work is being
done within the institution or by or in the physical
neighbourhood of a local authority. People who

have already been subjected to a bout of surveying about something else may not take kindly to being bombarded with questions about the library. This phenomenon is known as 'questionnaire fatigue'. Cynicism is another factor. People who complete questionnaires regularly for one or more organisations may become disillusioned if nothing seems to happen as a result of their co-operation. This usually results in comments in returned questionnaires like:

> 'I complained about this last year but you have not done anything about it'.

Timing of questionnaire administration is important. In public libraries October/November is preferred, failing which the Spring will do. If survey work involving visiting people's homes or interviewing in public places is intended the worst months of winter are best avoided. Interviewers should be issued with identification badges and it might be wise to inform the police of the intended work. In academic libraries the time chosen might relate to the nature of the work intended but the early part of the calendar year is a good time. Most categories of user are present and first year students have had a term or semester in which to become familiar with the library's services. There is also time to analyse and disseminate the results before the session ends. The coming of semesterisation, however, tends to make January a 'dead' month as students are either sitting examinations or are absent from the campus.

All service points (branch libraries, campus site libraries or whatever) should be surveyed to identify differences or problems particular to one or more sites. A large public library service with many branches may not be able to afford to survey them all simultaneously. In this case all branches should be surveyed in a three-year rotational period. Survey results from small branches should be interpreted with care as the number of returns may be so small as to make the results of limited worth. However it is a good idea to cross-check the results from different branches to try to identify similar patterns of activity. A variety of methods may be used to administer the questionnaires, depending on circumstances. In public libraries temporary staff can be hired if funds permit but it is often better to use existing library staff who will understand why the work is being undertaken and will be better qualified to explain and justify the exercise to users. The IPF manual offers precise instructions on how to administer the questionnaires. In academic and special libraries a range of options is available. Internal mail is an option open to both and can yield better results than postal questionnaires to people's home. While the former typically yields results of 15%-30%, internal mailing can double this response rate. In university libraries questionnaires can be administered both inside and outside the library. Sympathetic lecturers can be persuaded to distribute questionnaires at the beginning of lectures and if these are filled in at the time and collected at the end of the lecture there will be a good response rate. User education evaluation questionnaires can be distributed at the end of user education sessions and, again, if completed at the time, this will produce a good response rate. Within the library, staff are the best people to administer the questionnaire. They can distribute forms to users entering the library and explain the purpose of the study if questioned. It is a good idea to record the number of questionnaires distributed. From this it will be possible to calculate the response rate. At least 40% should be aimed for.

Questionnaires can be administered electronically and this can be done by mounting the questionnaire on the institution's web pages. It is important that the questionnaire is brought to the intended respondents' attention. This is easy if the questionnaire is administered in conjunction with a previously agreed activity like participating in a web-based learning programme. Failing that, the questionnaire could be presented as a default page on the institution's web pages so it is always brought to users' attention. A recently completed survey of the use of IT services at Glasgow Caledonian University Library offered the respondents the opportunity to complete the survey form either on paper or electronically. The return rate for the questionnaires administered on paper was about 14% while the return rate for the electronically administered questionnaire was 72%. The return rate might have been even higher had the IT skills of respondents been better. Time is saved in data analysis since the raw return data is already in electronic format and does not have to be created from scratch. This method, despite its advantages has one obvious and serious limitation. It effectively limits the sample to the computer literate and is most suitable for use in special libraries and universities with few non-traditional students. If used in public libraries it will tend to exclude the elderly and those with low skill levels.

The staffing and management of survey work is a perennial problem. Although library managers are keen to use survey results they are frequently reluctant to invest in the labour costs required. Some public and academic libraries maintain sections or departments with a remit for performance evaluation and research. They usually contain very few staff. Failing this, there may be a member of staff who monitors quality as part of his/her duties. Whoever manages survey work should be at a senior level, in order that he or she can contribute to the management process. There should also be adequate clerical support for checking completed questionnaires, preparing data for input, contributing to analysis and writing up etc. In higher education it is sometimes possible to use students who need to learn about survey work as part of their studies. However this will only work if the interests of students and librarians coincide. The future of staffing levels for evaluation is clearly linked to the development of initiatives like Best Value and the quality movement generally since they imply the need for quality officers.

Analysing the data and presenting results

In writing up and presenting the data it is tempting to discuss, in some detail, the methodologies chosen and how they were applied. It is best, however, to keep methodological description to a minimum and concentrate on results and recommendations for action. There should be only enough discussion of methodologies to allow others to repeat the survey and understand how the results were obtained. The audience for the completed report will include decision makers, both inside and outside the library, library staff and users of the service. They will be primarily interested in outcomes and recommendations for action especially insofar as they themselves are concerned.

Data can be analysed using a spreadsheet package such as Excel which will give adequate statistical analysis, in terms of totals and percentages for surveys of a moderate size (hundreds rather than thousands of returned forms). It can generate attractive ways of presenting the data like bar and pie charts. For very large surveys which are likely to be undertaken only occasionally it might be necessary to use a statistical package. One of the most frequently used is SPSS (Statistical Package for the Social Sciences). It has a large repertoire of statistical techniques and is well known to social researchers so it is fairly easy to get advice on its application.

There are two means of communication: closed and open. Closed communication includes written reports, newsletters and posters briefly summarising results. Open includes meetings of library staff, committee meetings and focus or other structured groups. All these will be appropriate in disseminating results. In public libraries the target audience will include service managers and library managers, local authority elected members and the general public. Summaries of the report, in press release form, can be sent to the local newspaper.

In special libraries, the report can be summarised in a house journal or newsletter if one exists and a copy of the report sent to the governing body. Similarly, universities maintain a range of publications including a staff journal or newsletter, a library newsletter and an alumni magazine. All these may be appropriate outlets. If the university students' union publishes its own newspaper this is a good way to communicate with undergraduates. Unfortunately it is much easier to communicate with full-time undergraduates than their part-time equivalents. Obviously submitting information to any publication outwith the library's control means loss of editorial control and it might be worth structuring key press releases to emphasise any points the library would like editors to take up.

Open communication offers the survey manager an opportunity to report on the survey in person and respond to comments and criticisms. Such feedback is a valuable supplement to the report and can contribute to future survey planning. It is a good idea to report to library staff as this gives them feedback on their own performance and how users view their work. Library committees and policy making bodies can also be approached. However, detailed reporting to a number of bodies can be extremely labour intensive and time consuming so this aspect of dissemination should be planned with that in mind.

Communication and feedback is in the process of being revolutionised by the development of email although this development naturally affects only those with access to a computer. However reporting results by email is quick, cheap because no mailing costs are involved and allows recipients to respond easily and quickly. It can be used in public libraries by users using the public library computers and in special and university libraries by users using the computers supplied by their employers. In higher education it is probably still more used to communicate with staff, rather than students but there is great developmental potential here.

3. Qualitative methods

On the whole qualitative methods are less used than quantitative methods. They figure less in the literature, especially standard textbooks, but, nevertheless, are increasingly reported and becoming better understood. Qualitative methods include such techniques as: interviews, frequently conducted on a one-to-one basis; meetings, whether loosely structured or more tightly organised, like focus groups; suggestions boxes; whether in manual or automated form (via an OPAC or website); observational methods and the keeping of diaries. Some involve direct, face-to-face interaction, and require special skills and training, others do not.

Qualitative methods work in two ways:

1)   Where you already know something about the subject. For example, if a survey indicates dissatisfaction with an aspect of the service without making clear the reasons why, it might then be appropriate to conduct interviews or hold a meeting with the people concerned to find out why they are dissatisfied.

2)   Where you do not fully understand the situation. Interviews or meetings could be held to ask 'why' -based questions to find out if a problem exists and what the performance issues are. If performance issues are identified they can be used either to tackle the problem or as a basis for collecting 'hard' quantitative

> data. The issues identified will help in the designing of the questionnaire.

Behind the qualitative method lies the simple concept of the story. We make sense of the world by telling one another stories. In talking about libraries we also talk about stories. What did the person come for? What were their intentions? What did they find? What happened? What was the value? (Van House 1995, p.7). The story can take many forms. A small child enthusing to its parents about a story hour at a public library is engaging in positive qualitative evaluation just as much as adult members of a focus group discussing a library service or participants in a structured interview. They all represent direct experience.

The qualitative approach has a number of characteristics and advantages. It works well with small samples and is appropriate for analysing problems in depth. For this reason it is useful for tackling complex and poorly understood problems. By collecting users' perspectives directly it is possible to tease out the underlying issues. Answering the question 'Why' rather than 'How often', emphasises the role of the participant who can present himself or herself as an actor in the events being studied. However the approach is much looser. It does not produce the tidy array of statistics at the end which a quantitative survey would and, for this reason, is perceived as being non-scientific. There is also a danger that it may be manipulated by vocal minorities who are good at casemaking. This sometimes happens with university teaching departments who are anxious to promote or retain a service which they see as benefitting them specifically. For this reason some background of quantitative data is desirable. This is not a problem for libraries which practise a systematic regime of assessment, but, for libraries not in that position, some background published sources such as LISU-produced figures might suffice. Qualitative methods also allow users to participate more in library management and give them a feeling that they are making a direct contribution to policy formulation.

It is often said that qualitative methods are less labour-intensive and time-consuming than quantitative methods. There is some truth in this. (The qualifications are discussed in detail below.) However, planning and facilitating meetings require special skills which library staff may not possess and the logistical problems of getting an appropriate group of people into a suitable room on a certain day at a certain time should never be underestimated. It helps considerably to have a pre-existing organisation, independent of the library, which acts as an organisational focus. The library at the University of Huddersfield has built up good relations with the University's Students Union which has 150 course representatives who can be called on for focus group work (Hart 1995, p.279). Glasgow Caledonian University had, for a time, an organisation called the Partnership for Quality Initiative which organised and facilitated meetings for several university departments, including the library. If no appropriate organisation exists it might be necessary to employ an outside body as Brent Arts and Libraries did when studying the needs of ethnic minorities within the borough (Batchelor & Tyerman 1994).

Focus groups

Of the various qualitative methods available the focus group is probably the one which has attracted most attention. They are called focus groups because the discussions start out broadly and gradually narrow down to the focus of the research. They are not a rigidly constructed question and answer session. Focus groups are used in a variety of situations. In business and industry they are often used to test new product ideas or evaluate television commercials. In higher education they can be used to 'float' new ideas such as embarking on a major fundraising venture. Focus groups, typically, consist of 8 to 12 people, with a moderator or facilitator who focuses the discussion on relevant topics in a non-directive manner. The role of the facilitator is crucial. He or she must encourage positive discussion without imposing control on the group. There is a danger that focus groups can degenerate into 'moan sessions'. The structured discussion group (also known as a *snowball* or *pyramid* discussion) (Wisdom 1995) is a variant on the focus group which tries to address this issue. After an introductory discussion the participants begin by working in small groups to identify and prioritise key themes. The groups then come together and each group is asked to make a point which is then tested with the other groups. Agreement is reached on each point in turn and a record is kept of the discussion which is verified towards the end of the session. Sessions last between 45 minutes and an hour and a quarter and about 14 points usually emerge.

Focus groups have several advantages over other forms of research which have been usefully summarised by Young (1993):

1) Participants use their own words to express their perceptions.

2) Facilitators ask questions to clarify comments.

3) The entire focus group process usually takes less time than a written survey.

4) Focus groups offer unexpected insights and more complete information.

5) In focus groups people tend to be less inhibited than in individual interviews.

6) One respondent's remarks often tend to stimulate others and there is a snowball effect as respondents comment on the views of others.

7) Focus group question design is flexible and can clear up confusing responses.

8) Focus groups are an excellent way to collect preliminary information.

9) Focus groups detect ideas which can be fed into questionnaire design.

There are 12 points to remember in organising focus groups:

1) Use facilitators from outside the library. Participants may be reluctant to discuss issues with a library facilitator and it is difficult for

a facilitator who has a vested interest in the outcome to be objective.

2) Select facilitators with expert skills. These include good communication skills and experience with group dynamics. They do not have to be an expert on the subject under discussion.

3) When recruiting ask for volunteers. A good way to do this is to add a brief section to regularly used questionnaires in which respondents are asked if they are willing to participate in further survey work. Relevant organisations which regularly collect opinion within the institution may also be able to help in providing names although this carries with it the risk of involving the 'rentacrowd' who are only too willing to express an opinion about anything.

4) Use stratified groups. In higher education separate staff from students and undergraduates from postgraduate students. Try to include all aspects of the target population such as full and part-time students.

5) Schedule 8-12 people per focus group, but always overschedule especially if working with undergraduates. Reminders by personal visits, telephone or prompting by lecturers may all be necessary in higher education. It is important to remember that Students' Representative Council members have many calls on their time and too much cannot be expected of them.

6) Allow ample time for discussion, usually up to two hours.

7) Develop a short discussion guide, based on the objectives of the research. This should be pre-tested on a sample population if possible. An experienced facilitator should be able to do much of this work.

8) If possible run three or four groups per target audience for the best results. One group may not provide enough data but organising more may be difficult.

9) Hold sessions in a centrally located, easily accessible room. Put up signs and notify colleagues who may be asked for directions. Ideally use a room with audio-taping facilities.

10) Reward participants for their time. Many libraries have no appropriate budget and a reward, in practice, often means nothing more than tea, coffee, biscuits and scones. Small rewards can be made in kind such as a free photocopying card or a book token donated by a bookseller. Such prizes can be allocated through a raffle.

11) In analysing and summarising the data look for trends or comments which are repeated in several sessions. Sessions can be analysed from audio tapes, flip chart paper and handwritten notes.

12) Don't overgeneralise information gained from focus groups and don't use it for policy decisions. Because of non-scientific sampling

and the inability to quantify results the information collected should be used carefully.

Practitioners have had varied experiences with focus groups. It is sometimes claimed (e.g. Hart 1995, p.280) that library staff should not be participants as this can inhibit other participants such as undergraduates. However I have never found students to have any inhibitions about criticising the library service in the presence of staff. Hart (1995) has organised seven focus groups over an academic year and, *inter alia*, makes the following points

1) The lunch period is a good time to hold them.

2) Each group lasted half an hour to an hour.

3) Misconceptions relating to all aspects of library organisation were widespread.

4) Focus groups are good for identifying problems which might not otherwise have been considered.

5) Focus groups are good for providing insights rather than answers.

6) Focus groups are not particularly cheap, mainly in terms of staff time which can be 3-4 hours per session.

Focus groups can reveal distinct gaps between the perceptions of library staff and those coming from the users. This is something librarians have to come to terms with if they are to benefit from the experience. Users might focus on a particular theme e.g. open access photocopying and binding facilities, and force library staff to rethink provision. Focus groups are usually a public relations success, as they show that the library is actively canvassing user opinion even if users' expectations of what the library can provide are sometimes unrealistic. Scheduling can be a real problem and if people cannot be recruited can threaten the result. Brent Arts and Libraries (Batchelor & Tyerman 1994), in its study of the needs of ethnic minorities, was unable to recruit sufficient people for the Afro-Caribbean focus group and it was impossible to recruit a focus group from among the business community because local traders were unwilling to give the necessary time. This was despite the fact that all participants were offered £10 each to attend. Nevertheless some 20 key service improvements were identified.

Focus groups are not very helpful in discussing technical issues because of lack of expertise among participants but it is important to recognise that the underlying issue may be valid even if presented in naive terms. For example a focus group on the use of a computer centre suggested a computer booking system, based on colour bands, as used in swimming pools. Even if the method was not very practical the need for a booking system was clearly identified. A somewhat unexpected advantage of focus groups is that they are an end in themselves. The very act of participating gives those present a feeling that they are 'having their say' and engaging in a form of two-way communication which helps to close the feedback loop.

Focus groups can be used with children but this is a highly specialised activity. They can be used with children from 7 to 16 years of age. Very simple questions should be asked and a 'chatty' manner is necessary. The use of pairs of friends encourages discussion and groups can then be built up consisting of up to three pairs. Parental consent for participation is needed, in writing wherever possible, up to the age of 16. Neutral venues are best, preferably a family home. Sessions can last up to 90 minutes provided the participants are interested, the facilitator is well-prepared and light refreshments are provided. As younger children (7-11) think concretely it is important to provide concrete examples like models and drawings and practical activities like drawing or writing down their ideas in the form of a postcard to a pen pal. For older participants (13+) bubble diagrams are a good method. A drawing of a simple situation includes a speech bubble and a thought bubble and respondents fill in what the people are thinking and saying. This is very useful for sensitive topics. A useful collection of methodologies for use with school pupils can be found in Nancy Everhart's *Evaluating the school library media center* (1998) which discusses evaluation methods with practical examples of questionnaires, interviews, focus groups, numbers gathering and observation. The practical difficulties of relating this work to children and young people are discussed.

Suggestions boxes

The suggestions box has been around for a long time and is now the subject of renewed interest in the present evaluation climate. The traditional 'suggestions box' in fact takes several physical forms. It might be a book, in which users can write suggestions, it might be a box, with an opening for inserting bits of paper on which comments are written or it could be pre-printed cards which can be completed by the user and analysed in a fairly structured way. About 10 academic libraries used this method in the mid 90s (Morgan 1995, p.60) and Essex Libraries is a public library example but there is uncertainty about what they are for: a public relations exercise or part of a customer care programme. Unless they are the latter they are largely a waste of time. The book or box must be prominently displayed and adequately publicised. It must be scrutinised regularly, preferably once a week and the issues raised identified. Two questions must be considered:

1)   Will the author of the suggestion receive an answer?

2)   Will the suggestion be acted upon or at least considered?

If the answer to both these questions is 'no' there is not much point in having a suggestions box, but to answer each question by letter could be a substantial clerical exercise.

There seems to be a good deal of user cynicism about the method. Suggestions are sometimes facetious or even obscene and, in the automated version described below a failure to respond rapidly can result in further questions, like:'Why does no one ever answer my questions?'.

Automated library systems have given a new lease of life to the suggestions box because some have question/answer facilities included in the OPAC.

Typically these include a screen on to which users can input questions and these are then answered by library staff. It is best if a specific member of staff has responsibility for this and ensures that all questions are answered promptly. In practice questions tend to be repetitive and the responsible staff member soon builds up expertise in replying to them. If the person who deals with the questions does not know the answer he or she can forward it to the relevant member of staff. The system should collect statistical data about questions, and may allow browsing and keyword searching. Regular overviewing of the questions makes it possible to identify performance issues and compare them with other sources of performance data. If the module contains a stop-word list of obscenities and offensive expressions these can be filtered out. These features make for a much more reliable evaluation tool than the manual suggestions box, mainly because feedback is much better. In practice questions tend to fall into two categories:

1) Precise questions specific to the enquirer e.g. 'If I do not return my books by a certain date will I have to pay a fine?

2) General questions about services which are easier to answer.

Generally speaking, the 'suggestions box', whether manual or automated, should be used in conjunction with other methods. The coming of the world wide web makes it possible to make suggestions services easily available over the Internet.

Diary techniques

Although the diary method is used by market and social researchers, in library and information science, its use seems to be largely confined to studying the activities of university undergraduates, mainly in respect of their study habits and use of library textbooks and other sources of information (Goodall 1994). It reflects many of the problems found in 'people' orientated research. Completing a diary can be viewed as a tedious task. While it might be possible to draw up a random sample of those to be approached it is likely that those who do agree to co-operate will be a small, self-selecting group. To be useful the diaries will have to be kept over a lengthy period but this is likely to lead to dropouts so a short period of a few days is more likely to produce satisfactory completion rates. The data obtained can be varied and highly specific but, for this very reason it can be extremely difficult to tease out performance issues from the detailed observations made. If diaries are kept over a long period errors can creep in and diarists who are aware that their writings are part of a structured research programme may begin to modify their observations, perhaps even unconsciously. Nevertheless they are a good way of collecting data which is difficult to collect in any other way, provided the data collected can be set in some sort of context.

Diary techniques are usually a less casual and unstructured activity than the term appears to imply. Although diaries allow users' actions and reactions to be recorded when they occur most people are not used to keeping a record of their activities and without a predetermined structure for recording the data is likely to be somewhat difficult to analyse. Diaries are usually structured and the respondent is given forms with checklists or performance issues prompting him or her to comment on the areas of study. It is important that the checklists are easy to understand otherwise the respondent may become confused. Such a method can remove the element of spontaneity and individuality which informs diary writing. Another method is a time diary which records the respondents' activities at different times of the day.

An example of diary research was carried out at the Centre for Research in Library and Information Management at the University of Central Lancashire as part of a wider study of library support for franchised courses in higher education (Goodall 1994). Approximately 120 first-year students were involved in the project which aimed to document the actual experience of students in relation to the provision and availability of library resources. Students were required to complete three or four diaries and attend a follow-up focus group discussion. Although the students received £25 each for participating there were difficulties in recruiting a sufficient sample and the project had to be vigorously promoted to attract sufficient interest. The result was a self-selected sample. Although there were problems in identifying suitable pieces of work for study, once assignments had been identified they provided issues on which to focus and gave a structure to the exercise. The diaries themselves were five-page A4 booklets, accompanied by guidelines and an example of a completed page. Time and place of work data was recorded and there were also coded tick boxes. There was also space for free comment.

The diaries were used to record materials consulted by students as they completed their assignments and also to note any difficulties they had in obtaining and/or using materials. The analysis of the diary entries then provided the framework for the focus group discussion in that it allowed the researcher to compile a list of themes and performance issues to use with the group. The students were encouraged to refer back to their diaries during the group discussion so that they were able to draw from specific examples to describe their actions in detail rather than talking in general terms. In this case then, the purpose of the diary project was two-fold:

1)   to record data
2)   to facilitate focus group discussion.

The diary data was more useful when set in a wider context of discussion.

Interviewing

Interviewing on a one-to-one basis is something that many librarians have done at one time or another. It is important to realise, however, that it is a structured activity and not just a chat. It can be seen as an extension of the meeting method, but by speaking to only one person it is possible to probe in detail into the experiences and reactions of respondents. For this reason it is a good method for exploring sensitive or confidential issues like library staff's relations with users. Interviewing is a skilled activity and because it is about the interaction between two people, well-developed social skills are essential. The interviewer must be good at getting people to talk. He or she should talk as little as possible and concentrate on listening. It is important to note the issues which the respondent raises and also those which are not raised. Unless the library can afford to employ paid interviewers, which is rarely the case, interviewing will probably be done by library staff. There is a danger that this might inhibit respondents or influence what they are prepared to say. Conversations can be recorded in notes or using a tape recorder. The latter method allows the interviewer to concentrate on what the respondent is saying but the tapes have to be transcribed or, at least analysed, which takes time (Slater 1990, pp.115-116).

There are three types of interview:

1) The structured or formal interview. This is based on a pre-prepared list of questions which are not deviated from. This closely resembles the administration of a questionnaire, except that the interviewer is present to explain and clarify questions.

2) The semi-structured interview. The interviewer works from a pre-prepared list of issues. The questions, derived from the issues, are likely to be open-ended to allow the respondent to express himself or herself.

3) The unstructured interview. In this case only the general subject is pre-determined and the interview is informal. This gives considerable

scope to the respondent to express his or her views but demands considerable skill on the part of the interviewer who must be able to subtly control digressions and tease out issues only partially examined by the respondent. (Morgan 1995, p.149). Interviewing is a skill which takes time to learn and is most needed for conducting unstructured interviews.

Observation

Observing what people are actually doing is a relatively little used technique in libraries but it has obvious attractions. It allows users to be observed in their natural setting and it makes it possible to study people who are unwilling or unlikely to give accurate reports on their own activity. The non-curricular use of computers in university libraries is a particularly good example of this. It also enables data to be analysed in stages or phases as understanding of its meaning is gained.

There are two types of observation, structured and unstructured.

1. Structured observation:

This is a predetermined activity where a form is used in which the observer records whether specific activities take place, when and how often. A well-designed data collection method will allow space to record unanticipated activity. However the form must be carefully designed at the outset to allow for most eventualities. Because this is essentially a statistical method it is usually considered to be a quantitative method.

2. Unstructured observation:

The observer records any behaviour or event which is relevant to the research questions being studied. This is a much more open-ended approach and as is the case with most qualitative research, is especially useful in exploratory research or where a situation is incompletely understood.

Observation, although on the face of it simple, is, in fact a highly skilled exercise, for the observer must know enough about the situation to understand and interpret what is going on. To return to the observation of computer use example, the observer can note important activity like mouse and keyboarding skills, file management and the expertise with which different software packages are being used but to do this the observer must be highly computer literate and be able to recognise and critically analyse and evaluate such activity. The methodology has some disadvantages. People who are aware they are being observed tend to change their behaviour, at least initially. There is an ethical question as observation without consent can be interpreted as an intrusion into privacy. It is not always possible to anticipate a spontaneous event and so be ready to observe and understand it. Not all events lend themselves to observation. The development of IT skills over a period of time is a good example. Observation can be very time-consuming and finally the subjectivity of the observer must be taken into account.

In making observations the researcher should focus only gradually on the research questions in order to open up possibilities for insight. The observer should also record his or her own subjective reactions to the events observed. This helps to distance the observer from them, an important way in which the questions of reliability and validity can be addressed. Notes should be made as close in time as possible to the events being recorded. Although in a library context unobtrusive observation is probably the norm the observer may also participate in the activities he or she is observing. To be a successful participant observer it is necessary to be approachable, friendly and receptive and to dress and behave appropriately (Gorman & Clayton, 1997. pp.104-106; 121-122). Observation is a particularly suitable technique for observing the use of electronic services like email, word processing and internet surfing or electronic information databases because precise quantitative instruments for evaluating them are still in the process of formation. It is technically possible to observe the use of a group of computers from a central point which makes reliable data collection easy as the users do not know they are being observed. However such a method necessarily raises ethical questions.

Qualitative research, generally, is a major research method in its own right and is useful for probing the sensitive issues which questionnaires do not deal with so effectively. As library and information science moves increasingly to the provision and use of electronic services so qualitative methods may become more attractive because so many poorly understood issues are arising which cannot be addressed with the precision that quantitative methods require.

4. Pitfalls and Progress

The conclusion of a piece of survey work does not necessarily mark the end of the exercise. The results should include recommendations for action but a number of factors may affect the outcomes of the study and may even lead to their modification.

1) The problem may be insoluble for a variety of reasons. Resources may be unavailable to tackle it. The study may show that a particular group of users requires particular attention but money may not be available to undertake the work needed. It may be difficult to collect information on which to base decision-making as the Brent study showed. If the co-operation and support of departments outwith the library is needed, e.g. manual staff support for extended opening hours, it may be difficult to proceed, but at least, solid data is available for making a case.

2) More questions may be raised than answered. This is often the case with short overview surveys which may raise puzzling issues that require further investigation. One group of users may be much less satisfied with the service than others. It may be necessary to mount a further study of the group to find out why.

3) Misconceptions are an unavoidable problem. Users' comments on survey forms and at meetings can show that they have inaccurate perceptions or have fallen victim to rumours. Sometimes the numbers, e.g. all the students on a particular course,

can be substantial. The consequences, in the form of angry letters to local newspapers, or articles in student magazines, can be serious and it may be necessary to mount a PR exercise to clarify the situation. Sometimes these errors can be accepted at quite a high level. I have found evidence of quite senior academics credulously accepting unfounded rumours.

4) Contradictory results sometimes occur. These may be the results of faulty methodology or paying too much attention to pressure from vocal interest groups. Building on experience over a period of years, comparisons with similar institutions, and using a regime of assessment which consists of a range of methods are the best ways of avoiding these problems.

5) The results of the study may generate criticism. This may be criticisms of methodologies or outcomes. Following proper procedures is the best way to avoid criticisms of methodology. Outcomes may be criticised if they are perceived as having deleterious implications. For example, the recommendation to deskill a service, previously run by professional staff, may not be well received by those concerned. This can result in delaying, modifying, or even abandoning the proposals.

6) The information collected from a survey can go out-of-date quite quickly. The current move to electronic information services is changing expectations rapidly and this must be allowed for. It may be necessary to look at the same problem areas on a regular basis to identify new and changing needs.

7) As implied in (6) above the performance issues which inform evaluation must be regularly reviewed to ensure that the changing needs of users are being addressed.

Over a period of years of years it should be possible to develop a systematic regime of evaluation composed of questionnaire work, formal qualitative methods like focus groups and other meetings, ancillary methods such as suggestion boxes and comparisons with other departments within the institution. A range of performance measures will emerge, some recurring, others needing consideration less frequently. These will require evaluation and comparisons should be made with similar institutions and existing data to get an idea of context. Research-based methods which seek to identify performance issues objectively have been developed in the 1990s.

On the basis of this strategy it will be possible to pass through a hierarchy of quality, composed of the following elements:

1) Recognising the need: identifying areas of ignorance within the library.

2) Find out what users need.

3) Adapting services to respond to their needs.

4) Developing comparisons with other libraries.

5) Understanding users' needs in a comparative perspective.

If it proves possible to move through all five stages then it might be possible to consider benchmarking as a further qualitative step (Town 1995). Benchmarking has been variously described as 'a systematic approach to business improvement where best practice is sought and implemented to improve a process beyond the benchmark performance' and 'stealing shamelessly'. It is a technique developed by industry in which best practice by one's competitors is studied to improve one's own performance. Benchmarking can improve the customer focus through seeing how others satisfy their customers and in librarianship libraries can compare themselves with each other and relevant service industries with a view to an all-round improvement in performance. It is, however, difficult to compare services in different institutions which are highly qualitative like the Enquiries service. Measures or benchmarks to use in comparing libraries have to be chosen and it can be difficult to find several libraries for which the same set of measures will be appropriate. Obviously the best benchmarking partners have to be chosen to give the exercise credibility.

Benchmarking is no longer a marginal activity. About 40% of British academic libraries are involved in benchmarking in some way and in Australia the figure is at least 50%. SCONUL has conducted six benchmarking pilots focusing on the following areas: advice and enquiry desks, information skills training, counter services and library environment. Although these pilots have been useful it has proved difficult to devise generally acceptable measures and because of ethical and confidentiality issues outcomes have not featured a great deal in the literature. Enquiry work has emerges as a favourite theme for benchmarking and this has cropped up in public libraries too. In

1997 four public library authorities: Berkshire, Brent, Kent and Westminster co-operated on a study of enquiry services (Spiller 1998, p. 76). The survey divided into three parts. A 'customer survey' was found to be of limited value because expressed levels of satisfaction were very high. An 'unobtrusive testing ' phase categorised answers given to enquiries as 'complete and correct/ partially correct/ wrong' and the referral process into various levels of correctness or inappropriateness. A third stage developed process maps for all the stages and factors involved in the enquiry chain. The unobtrusive testing process identified a number of 'incorrect' or 'partially correct' answers and particular problems with the referral process, staple problems with enquiry work, in fact. Measures were taken to rectify problems. Again issues of confidentiality arose. Bohme and Spiller (1999, pp. 208-217) reprint the documentation used including the questions asked and the unobtrusive monitoring forms.

5. Case Studies and Future Developments

This chapter looks at examples of interesting practice in public, academic and special libraries. It considers survey work, charters and service level agreements and examples of relevant research projects.

Survey work in public libraries

Among the issues which can be explored in public library user surveys are (Spiller 1998, pp. 74-77):

- user practice (e.g. frequency of visits, types of use)
- user capabilities (e.g. ability to use computer catalogues)
- user motivations (e.g. reasons for use)
- user satisfaction (with different aspects of service)
- user opinions (e.g. preferences for future service development).

Examples include:

Hackney user survey

Aslib and Solon Consultants carried out the survey for Hackney Libraries in 1995 and the information was used to radically reshape the authority's libraries by reducing some service points and strengthening others. It was possible to do this because the public's views had been sought. Among the data collected was 'reasons for borrowing'. The largest percentage 43% was 'read for pleasure' with 'education' following at 21%. 'Acquire knowledge' was 16% with 'recreations and pastimes at 13%. 'Work' accounted for only 7% so, for the majority of users, the library was a recreational service.

Bromley exit survey

This survey was carried out for Bromley Libraries by Capital Planning Information Ltd. Nine different library sites were surveyed. A question about user capabilities – *Are you able to use the library computer catalogue unaided?* – produced a worrying 'no' response rate of 45%. Users were also asked about services that they might like to use in the future such as access to PCs and the Internet. Responses produced a clear age range split with the youngest being most enthusiastic about such services and the oldest being least interested.

Survey of Birmingham Central Library

This survey, undertaken in 1996, was a follow-up to a previous survey done in 1992. This allowed the authority to monitor the effectiveness of action taken to remedy previously identified problems. A number of service aspects showed improvement:

- time spent waiting
- ease of finding books
- study/reading places
- helpfulness of signing.

However a range of new problems caused over 20% dissatisfaction:

- the range of books and other stock
- temperature levels
- noise levels
- quality of equipment.

These issues are the staples of any large library and the identification of new problems shows the need for repeat surveys at regular intervals.

Sandwell lapsed user survey

This survey, carried out in 1997, reflects public librarians' increasing preoccupation with the penetration of library services into the community. Non-use is an increasingly important issue for all types of library and here, public librarians seem to be giving a lead. Completed postal questionnaires were received from 138 library members who had not borrowed material in the previous three years. The results were fairly reassuring. Many respondents had used the library. They were lapsed borrowers rather than users. However, in response to the question – *Have you made use of the library service since you joined?* – only 25% replied 'regularly' while 65% replied 'a few times'. The remaining 10% had used the service only once or not at all.

Non-borrower types of use in the previous year were:

- reference materials   18%
- visited with children   17%
- photocopier   12%

- personal study   10%
- chose books for others   7%
- read newspapers/mags   6%

The use of outside consultants in some of these studies is interesting.

A list of priorities for future surveys might include:

Topics

- impact (quantitative measures)
- costing by function
- market penetration (lapsed/non users)
- promotion of services
- book buying compared with borrowing.

Services

- information/enquiries
- audio/visual services
- electronic information sources.

East Renfrewshire Council Library survey 1999

In 1999 East Renfrewshire Council (1999) undertook its first study of its 10 branch libraries. Other Council departments, including recreational services undertook parallel surveys. The questionnaire (see Figure 1) included 12 rateable performance issues including four which would come under the general heading of environment. Helpfulness of staff, stock, audio-visual materials, information services, computer services, photocopying and opening hours were other issues. Across the branches 'helpfulness of staff' received high ratings, between 88 and 98% rating the service good.

Cultural Services Division
Community and Leisure Department
GIFFNOCK LIBRARY

Please take a few moments to tell us what you think about our facilities. We are very keen to improve our services and your answers can help us achieve this.

Date of visit ....   Time of visit ....

	good	fair	poor	not used
general appearance and decor	☐	☐	☐	☐
lighting	☐	☐	☐	☐
cleanliness	☐	☐	☐	☐
heating and ventilation	☐	☐	☐	☐
helpfulness of staff	☐	☐	☐	☐
choice of fiction	☐	☐	☐	☐
choice of non-fiction	☐	☐	☐	☐
choice of audio visual	☐	☐	☐	☐
quality of information	☐	☐	☐	☐
computer reference/catalogue system	☐	☐	☐	☐
photocopying equipment	☐	☐	☐	☐
convenience of opening times	☐	☐	☐	☐

Have you noticed any changes in the quality of the service provided over the past year or so?

     improved ☐   no change ☐   poorer ☐

What do you like best about the service? ....
....

What do you dislike most? ....
....

Any suggestions on how we can improve things? ....
....

Are you aware of the Let us Know system which gives you the opportunity to comment, suggest or complain about any of the services provided by East Renfrewshire Council using pre-paid leaflets?

       I am aware ☐   I am not aware ☐

Figure 1 – East Renfrewshire Council Library questionnaire

Fiction stock fared less well with typical 'good' ratings of between 51 and 82%. Ratings for audio visual stock were even poorer ranging typically from 14 to 42%. Information resources received good ratings, typically between 51 and 86% of respondents rating this service good but the computer catalogue and computer reference services fared worse, perhaps because of high levels of non-use. The problems with audio-visual and computer services match two of the survey priorities for public libraries listed above: audio-visual services and electronic information resources. Two fundamental issues stand out: quality of staff and quality of stock. It is interesting that the views of the Scottish suburban general public and those of north German academic library users (see below) are so similar. The questionnaire also asked users if they were aware of the Councils' Let us Know system which gives them an opportunity to make comments, suggestions and complaints about the service provided. Only one branch produced an 'awareness' rating of more than 50%, an indication that, laudable as the aim of open communication may be, it can be difficult to achieve.

PUBLIC LIBRARY
National Standard User Survey

This survey is collecting information to measure the quality of library services. After you have used the library, <u>please will you complete this form and return it as you leave</u>.

1. Tick all those boxes which show what you did during today's visit to this library:

☐ Borrow/return*book(s)*or renew   ☐ Borrow/return cassette(s)

☐ Borrow/return compact disc(s)   ☐ Borrow/return video(s)

☐ Read newspaper(s)/magazine(s)   ☐ Seek information/find some thing out

☐ Use the photocopier   ☐ Browse

☐ Sit to study or work   ☐ See exhibition or event

☐ Something else .... Please say what _____

If you did not come to the library today to borrow a book please go straight to Q5.

2. How many books did you borrow from the library today? _____

3. <u>If you were seeking a particular book(s)</u> during today's visit, please write <u>either</u> the TITLE <u>or</u> SUBJECT <u>or</u> AUTHOR of up to 3, and show if you were able to obtain them: (see examples below)

	Yes	No	No, but did Reserve a book
_____	☐	☐	☐
_____	☐	☐	☐
_____	☐	☐	☐

Examples: TITLE: Gone with the Wind, SUBJECT: Gardening, AUTHOR: Dick Francis

4. <u>If you came</u> to the library today <u>without a particular book in mind</u>, did you find one to borrow?   Yes ☐   No ☐

5. <u>If you came</u> to the library <u>to seek information</u>:

	Yes	Partially	No
i. did you get the information you needed?	☐	☐	☐
ii. did you consult a member of staff?	☐		☐

6. <u>If you came for</u> a Cassette(s), CD(s), or Video(s), did you borrow any? Only tick a box if you intended to borrow such an item.

	Yes	No	No, but did Reverse an item
Music cassette(s)	☐	☐	☐
Talking Book(s) incl. language courses	☐	☐	☐
Comapct disc(s)	☐	☐	☐
Video(s)	☐	☐	☐

Figure 2 – Public Library National Standard User Survey

78

Institute of Public Finance (IPF) Public Library User Survey (Plus)

This national standard for user surveys grew out of the Audit Commission's Citizens' Charter exercise in 1992. There was a strong feeling that conventional statistics were not adequate to assess how well libraries provided materials and information to the public. Surveys of users which asked specific questions seemed to be the answer. Following a large scale pilot in 1993 and follow-up work, overseen by the Committee on Public Library Statistics, a National Standard for undertaking surveys of users in UK public libraries was launched in late 1994. This establishes a common base on which library authorities can compare their results and a forum for the development of visitor surveys (England & Sumsion 1995, pp.109-110). The Standard, available from the IPF, takes the form of a manual of instructions, advice and background information on the survey with appendices. The appendices contain worked examples of the documentation and samples of the types of analysis which could be undertaken on the data gathered. Software is also provided. After the data has been collected analysis can be done inhouse, by an outside consultancy or the IPF. Participating authorities can compare results at service point level within their own authority, against service points in another authority of their choice or compare purely at the authority level, depending on the type of survey chosen. The questionnaire (see Figure 2) contains 'core' questions. Additions to the core questions can be made in collaboration with the IPF. There are a number of supplementary questions which some authorities have added that can be used by others.

Leeds Library and Information Services conducted its first major user survey in December 1994, based on IPF's Public Libraries User Survey (Plus) (Pritchard 1995). The availability of the survey resolved uncertainties about what questions to ask, sampling tables and how to collate the data. The documentation provided covered all aspects of how to set up and run the survey. Apart from the data itself the fact that statistically valid data was collected was seen to be a major benefit.

Currently, 92 public library authorities subscribe to the scheme and well over 200,000 surveys are recorded on the IPF database. Members can compare their local results against published national averages. A children's survey was launched in 1998 following extensive piloting and a PLUS sub group has been formed to investigate community surveys. The core areas covered by the CIPFA PLUS questionnaire are: user activities in the library; number of books borrowed; a needs fill question; user satisfaction relating to a number of services; frequency of visits; sex, age and occupation of respondent and postcode area of the respondent a feature which makes it possible to calculate distance travelled to the library (Spiller 1998, p. 72).

Academic libraries

In survey work, university libraries are also moving towards standardisation, albeit in a less struc-

---

**POPPLETON METROPOLITAN UNIVERSITY
LIBRARY SERVICES**

General Satisfaction Survey

Please help us improve library services by answering a few questions

1. What did you do in the library today? For each, please circle the number that best reflects how successful you were.
How successful

	Completely		Not successful		Did not do at all	
Looked for books or periodicals	5	4	3	2	1	0
Studied	5	4	3	2	1	0
Reviewed current literature	5	4	3	2	1	0
Did a literature search (manual or computer)	5	4	3	2	1	0
Asked a reference question	5	4	3	2	1	0
Browsed	5	4	3	2	1	0
Returned books	5	4	3	2	1	0
Other (What?)	5	4	3	2	1	0

2. How many items (books, periodicals, or papers etc) <u>did you use</u> in the library today but <u>did not borrow</u>? ☐ (number)

3. How long did you stay in the library today?___ hours___minutes___

4. How <u>easy</u> was the library to use <u>today</u>? (Circle one):
    Not at all easy   1   2   3   4   5   Very easy

Why?_____

5. Overall, how <u>satisfied</u> are you with <u>today's</u> library visit? (Circle one):
    Not at all easy   1   2   3   4   5   Very easy

Why?_____

6. Today's visit was <u>primarily</u> in support of (Tick one)
    1. Coursework ☐ 3. Teaching ☐ 5. A mix of several purposes ☐
    2. Research   ☐ 4. Current awareness ☐ 6. Other: _____ ☐

7. You are? (Tick)
    A full time   or part time   student
    1. Undergraduate   ☐ 3. Teaching staff ☐ 5. Other staff ☐
    2. Graduate student ☐ 4. Research staff ☐ 6. Other:_____

8. Your School or Department:_____

*Figure 3 – Poppleton Metropolitan University Library Services
General Satisfaction Survey*

GLASGOW CALEDONIAN UNIVERSITY LIBRARY
Annual Satisfaction Survey

Please help us to monitor and improve library services by answering a few questions

1. Please look at the statements below and circle the number beside each one which best reflects your experience **during today's (or recent) visit**

	Did not do today	Strongly disagree				Strongly agree
The Library staff were helpful	0	1	2	3	4	5
Noise and comfort levels were satisfactory	0	1	2	3	4	5
The opening hours met my needs	0	1	2	3	4	5
I found my way round the Library without difficulty	0	1	2	3	4	5
I found the Electronic Catalogue easy to use	0	1	2	3	4	5
The books and periodicals I wanted were available on the shelves	0	1	2	3	4	5
The photocopiers were in good working order	0	1	2	3	4	5
My information/reference enquiry was answered helpfully	0	1	2	3	4	5
The Library provided access to the electronic information resources that I needed	0	1	2	3	4	5
The Library communicates well with its users e.g. publicity materials, signs, user education	0	1	2	3	4	5

2. On the whole I was satisfied with today's **(or recent visit)** to the Library

	0	1	2	3	4	5

3. Today's **(or recent visit)** visit was primarily in support of **(please tick one only)**

   1. Coursework ☐   2. Research ☐
   3. Teaching ☐   4. Other ☐

4. You are **(please tick one only)**

   1. Full time undergraduate ☐   2. Part time undergraduate ☐
   3. Taught post graduate student ☐   4. Teaching staff ☐
   5. Researcher ☐   6. External ☐
   7. Other ☐

5. Your Faculty **(please tick one only)**

   1. Health ☐   2. Science and Technology ☐
   3. Business ☐   4. Other ☐

6. Your campus **(please tick one only)**

   1. City ☐   2. Park ☐

Figure 4 – Glasgow Caledonian University Library
General Satisfaction Survey

tured and coherent fashion, and in this *Measuring academic library performance* Van House et al (1990) has been influential. The Follett report suggested that the user satisfaction survey it contained could be used in Britain in a suitably amended form. Adapting US academic library standard forms to British practice has several advantages (Revill 1995). They have been validated by practice, they make it unnecessary to invent one's own, they allow comparisons of user satisfaction between sites and years and they permit inter-institutional comparisons. With the help of volunteers SCONUL piloted five questionnaires, covering different aspects of library service in early 1995. The questionnaires were:

1)   general user satisfaction
2)   quality of service
3)   availability of materials
4)   enquiries and reference services
5)   stock selection.

The Library of the University College of Swansea has used the Van House originals, independently of the SCONUL initiative and Glasgow Caledonian University Library has used the Van House general user satisfaction survey in an increasingly modified form. Figure 3 is an example of a modified proforma, derived from Van House by SCONUL and apparently originating from the mythical Poppleton Metropolitan University so beloved *of Times Higher Educational Supplement* readers.

As a result of various research initiatives a modified version of the Van House user satisfaction survey questionnaire was devised at Glasgow Caledonian University. The performance issues in section one are derived from these initiatives. The list of issues reflected in section 1 of the Van House questionnaire had not been found to be very relevant and the questionnaire proved difficult to analyse satisfactorily. The Glasgow Caledonian questionnaire was successfully administered in 1995 and 1996 and has undergone further modifications since (see Figure 4). It permits inter-site, inter-faculty and inter-user group comparisons. There is space on the back for comments which produces qualitative data which can be compared with the quantitative data also collected. The survey has been administered over a five year period (1995-1999 inclusive) and now provides a longitudinal perspective on how the services have developed over that time.

If universities as a whole regularly survey their teaching, learning and central services the university library is surveyed, probably annually, as part of this process. This gives the library an opportunity to compare itself with other services provided by the University. The practice is not widespread but the University of Central England in Birmingham is a good example. The University of Central England maintains a Centre for Research into Quality, one of whose functions is to conduct an annual university-wide student satisfaction survey. The 1998 annual report, University of Central England (1998) covered central services like library and computing services and word processing facilities, refectories and student services as well as course organisation, teaching staff and teaching and learning. The survey is based on a lengthy questionnaire which, in 1998, included the views of nearly 2000 respondents and provided more than a million items of information. The section on the library extends over 16 pages and is more comprehensive than many stand-alone inhouse library surveys. As academic libraries are now major providers of computing facilities the sections on word processing and computing facilities are also relevant. The 1998 survey recorded high levels of user satisfaction especially with staff helpfulness. The annual surveys have been ongoing since 1991 and a number of familiar issues have emerged over this period: range of books; up-to-dateness of books; availability of recommended course material; multiple copies of core books; range of journals; opening hours; availability of study places and noise levels. Perhaps predictably availability of recommended course material and multiple copies of core books are the main areas of dissatisfaction. The Centre also undertakes specialist surveys and this has included the library. The Centre recognises the need to close the feedback loop and goes to considerable lengths to publicise the outcomes of its work.

There are advantages and some disadvantages to this method. One can be certain the survey has been carried out expertly and that the data is reliable and comparisons within the university are possible. However the data collected is limited so there will still be a need for specialist surveys. The library, although it benefits from the process has no direct control over it. However, studies such as this are increasingly helpful, partly because they include IT issues and partly because they point to performance issues which are common to both the library and other services as well.

A European example

The library of the University of Munster in north western Germany is one of the most active in Germany in evaluation and performance measurement. It conducted a survey of user satisfaction in 1982 and repeated the exercise in 1996 (Buch 1997). Perhaps, because of the relative infrequency of surveying, it was a substantial and methodologically complex exercise. After the initial survey design it was pre-tested on 30 users. This raised problems with jargon, especially abbreviations and the questionnaire was modified. The completed questionnaire comprised a total of 52 questions in 19 different service areas. The survey was carried out over one complete week in January from 8 am to 9 p.m. each day and was administered by 4 librarians and 2 student assistants. The questionnaire was administered to 8 subjects per hour who took, on average, 20 minutes to complete the form. This led the surveyors to conclude that the questionnaire should have been shorter. A total of 578 usable questionnaires were completed and analysed by Excel. Because the comments written on the form had to be classified and coded data preparation and analysis took until the following May. The analysis of the quantitative data took approximately 130-140 hours and the analysis of the qualitative data took another 50 hours, about 190 hours in total.

Among the results was a strong desire for longer opening hours which resulted in extended Saturday opening. Overall user satisfaction was high although satisfaction with the stock was lower. The most highly rated area was 'helpfulness of staff'. The surveyors were surprised to discover, that the Internet which appeared to be a 'favourite toy' was unfamiliar to 76% of users. Publicity for this service was increased. The survey results were publicised by an exhibition and a press conference.

Clearly the labour costs of such a large survey are substantial and the time taken to analyse qualitative comments is particularly noteworthy. The issues raised will be familiar to many academic librarians outside Germany.

Special libraries

Surveying special libraries is rather different from public and academic libraries because of the small number of users involved. This makes it possible to do a census rather than a survey. Because of the frequent availability of internal mailing, either paper or electronic, it is often possible to get a high response rate but, even so, the absolute numbers dealt with will not be very great. Because of this it is possible to use a questionnaire which mixes quantitative and qualitative elements and because of the high level of commitment of users it is acceptable to make the questionnaire quite long. The library of the Scottish Agricultural Sciences Agency completed an unpublished survey of its library use in

January 1996. The questionnaire was six pages long. It was divided into four sections:

1) Visiting the library.
2) Services provided.
3) Quality of service.
4) Future.

There was a total of 23 questions, a mixture of closed and open, the latter giving the respondents adequate opportunity to make qualitative observations. A total of 149 questionnaires were sent out and 74 were returned (49.6%). Statistical data was generated using Excel. Satisfaction with the service given was very high, although inevitably misconceptions surfaced. Perhaps not surprisingly in a special library, journal circulation was the most controversial issue. Journals also figured prominently in replies to the question on better services. Conclusions from the questionnaire included the need for better library promotion and the impact of IT, issues not confined to special libraries.

The British Ministry of Defence operates a comprehensive programme of evaluation which includes user survey reports for each library in the Ministry of Defence HQ Information and Library service. There is also a rolling programme of six monthly surveys aimed at giving a satisfaction performance indicator. The aim is to achieve 90% satisfaction against three key performance indicators: 'Speed'; 'Information provided' and 'Courteous and helpful'. To date these targets have all been achieved. Indeed the 'Courteous and helpful' indicator regularly scores 100%. Characteristically the problems of getting customer feedback in a special library means that the number of respondents is small, between 300 and 350. One of the outcomes of the evaluation programme was a Library Service Charter which includes a commitment to monitoring and customer feedback.

Charters and service level agreements

The Citizen's Charter was launched by the then Prime Minister, John Major, in June 1991. Its stated aims are to improve quality, choice and value in public services by publishing standards which the public should expect, and by establishing a system for redress where standards are not met. The principles of public service listed in the Charter are:

1) Standards which are explicit and published.
2) Openness and accountability.
3) Information which is readily available.
4) Choice.
5) Non-discrimination.
6) Accessibility.
7) Systems for complaint and redress.

Local authorities were listed among the public services covered so the implications for public libraries were obvious. Higher education was not mentioned specifically but the impact has, nevertheless, been substantial. The Citizen's Charter's first principle of public service, Standards, establishes the link with local customer charters:

'Every citizen is entitled to expect explicit standards, published and prominently displayed at the point of delivery. These standards should invariably include courtesy and helpfulness from staff, ... and a commitment to prompt action, which might be expressed in terms of a target response or waiting time.'

The challenge was swiftly taken up. By August 1992 at least 13 authorities had published a library charter and some 14 others were working towards one. Although these varied in length, style, organisation and detail, they shared common concerns about accessibility, appropriateness, quality and value for money. They offered a mixture of commitments and pledges, some general, some specific, and some supported by numeric standards. Few exhibited a link between market research and the charter pledges (Library Association 1992).

Also in 1991, a government minister challenged the Library Association to produce a model charter for libraries which appeared in 1993 (Library Association 1993). It includes a commitment to involve the community, undertake surveys regularly and to publish a Statement of Standards covering all areas of the service. There is a section on access covering opening times, signing and publicising, and access for those with special needs. There are also sections on Environment and facilities, Books and other stock, Information Services, Staff, Encouraging people to use the services and Monitoring the services. This was supplemented by a *Model statement of standards* (Library Association 1995) which covers specifics e.g.: 20 minute travelling time to service points; provision for people with physical disabilities, signing and guiding, minimum opening hours, time taken to attend to users and answer telephones, provision for children, seating and health and safety standards, minimum stock and information services provision, minimum numbers of, and performance of staff, marketing and evaluation. This mentions specifically annual surveys, suggestions boxes and answers to complaints.

These two documents have given public libraries a valuable basis on which to proceed. By May 1995, 52 authorities had charters and a further 16 were preparing them. Public library charters are usually attractively produced, sometimes in A5 leaflet form and printed in two or more colours to attract attention to them. The City of Westminster initially produced separate charters for libraries and archives but has now abandoned these in favour of a single document entitled *Service standards and promises*. This describes services simply and explains in fairly general terms what standard of services users can expect. There is a promise to listen to comments, respond to complaints and conduct surveys. There is also a short section explaining how users can help the library. In 1997 the Library Association's Branch and Mobile Libraries Group published its own specialised charter *Charter for public mobile library services*. It is based upon *A charter for public libraries* and the *Model statement of standards* and includes such specialised issues as stopping times, the need to review routes frequently and the role of mobile libraries in community information provision.

In higher education the position is rather different. Academic libraries are under less pressure to produce charters and consequently fewer have done so. However there are several influences, both direct and indirect. There are general higher education charters for England and Scotland and the National Union of Students has developed a student charter which, inter alia, states that students should have 'the right to effective learning supports'. Some universities have produced general charters. Liverpool John Moores University produced the first of these in 1993. It is divided into specific sections which include a short item about the library. The overall statements and promises can affect the library even if it is not mentioned specifically e.g. provision of feedback to students, involving students in the decision making process, provision of a suitable learning environment and the complaints procedure. Of the specific library charters one of the most attractively produced is that of the University of London Library. It is printed in two colours in A5 leaflet form. It was produced in early 1994 and has been kept short intentionally to give it a long shelf life although changes to practice probably imply updating. It outlines in six points what a reader has a right to expect from the service. Detail is available in the Library's range of leaflets. It covers Service Delivery and Customer Care, Quality (which includes a reference to surveys), Collections, Information Technology, The Working Environment and Complaints Procedure. The most detailed is that produced by Sheffield Hallam University Library which is a detailed document extending over four sheets of A4. It is divided into eight sections: Access, Accommodation, Materials, Information Services,

Photocopying and Sales, Audio Visual Services, Communicating with Students and Student Responsibilities. It makes promises on specific issues e.g. responding to 75% of enquiries immediately and 95% photocopier operational availability. What distinguishes higher education charters, both general and library specific, is that they tend to be contracts in that they specify the behaviours expected from the students in return for the services promises. Public library charters do not usually have a contractual element.

It is fair to say that there has been a good deal of cynicism about charters. They can be seen as bland promises, merely rephrasing institutional policy or 'weasel words' which make impressive statements but do not promise anything measurable. They can also be seen as a passing fad and, if they descend to specifics, can go out of date. They can become an end in themselves, unrelated to the realities of

Figure 5 (opposite) – Open Polytechnic of New Zealand Student Library Service Charter

Open Polytechnic of New Zealand
Student Library Service Charter

The Student Library Service exists to assist you in your study. Customer service is our primary focus and drives all our work processes. We recognise the difficulties faced by distance students and will provide access to information by:

- *lending material recommended in courses,*
- *undertaking subject searches to support your assessment work,*
- *offering bibliographies and*
- *providing other learning support such as study skills information.*

Communication

- We will maintain a courteous and helpful manner.
- We will be available to take phone calls in person between 8.30am and 5.00pm Monday to Friday.
- Phone calls will be answered within five rings.
- We will clear email, voice mail and fax messages during the working day on which they are received.
- We invite your comments and suggestions about our services.
- If you have an issue which you cannot resolve with the person you are dealing with, you may request to speak to the Student Library Librarian.

Referrals

- When we receive a request that is outside the scope of our service we will pass it on to the appropriate person, immediately where possible, and always within one working day of receiving it.
  We will notify you of the name and contact details of the person to whom we have passed your request.

Response Times

- When an item is available in the Library, it will be sent from the Library within one working day of your request being received.
- When an item is not available in the Library, notification of delay or alternatives will be sent from the Library within one working day of your loan request being received.
- When an item is not available in the Library and you elect to wait for that item, every effort will be made to send it within two weeks.
- We will send information or material from the Library within three working days of your subject search request being received.

Equity of Access

- We will purchase multiple copies of all items listed as *recommended reading* in course material in order to make copies of these available for you to borrow.
- We will shorten the loan period when items are under heavy demand, in order to ensure the maximum availability of items.
- We will send you material, within New Zealand, by courier or FastPost, at no direct cost.
- We will provide you with copies of recommended journal articles at no direct cost.
- Within New Zealand, a freephone and free fax line are provided for you to contact the Library.

the service and they can be difficult to get right. There is also concern as to whether they are legally binding. To be successful they should be both the outcome of evaluation, offering objectively deliverable promises and they should also be seen as a part of a continuing evaluation process. There is no doubt that the specific promises they often contain on feedback and surveying have boosted the evaluation movement. If well designed and kept up to date charters can:

1) improve communications with users

2) demonstrate a commitment to quality

3) focus staff attention on performance issues.

Although charters have been viewed as a mid-90s fad they have not gone away in higher education. There seems to be two reasons for this:

1. The growth of student numbers in higher education has resulted in many people coming to university who come from family backgrounds with no previous experience of higher education and have no idea of what to realistically expect of higher education services. This has led to a need for expectation management and a charter is a good way of doing this.

2. The growth of off-campus and work-based learning which results in irregular user contact with the library. In such circumstances laying out the ground rules is a good idea.

Glasgow Caledonian University library's charter, introduced in September 1999, is a good example of a charter inspired by the need for expectation management as library staff felt they needed a document which would clearly define the respective rights and obligations of library staff and users. The draft was circulated to all library and all other university staff for comment and discussed with the Students Association before being presented to the University's Learning and Teaching Committee for final amendment and approval. The Students Association obligingly printed it in full in their *Students handbook* which is circulated to all new students at the beginning of the academic year. Copies were also posted to all new students as part of their university starter pack. The Open Polytechnic of New Zealand (1998) has charters for both staff and students. The development of the student charter (see Figure 5) was affected by the status of the Open Polytechnic of New Zealand as a distance learning organisation and the need to supply books and information to remote users receives greater prominence than in a conventional charter.

Special libraries too, have charters and the Ministry of Defence HQ Information and Library Service (1998) *Library service charter* is a good example. It extends over six pages and, as well as charter statements has sections on services, service targets, customer feedback and complaints procedures. As with higher education charters it lists the duties and rights of staff and customers in much the same way that higher education charters list the duties and rights of both staff and students. The charter statements stick mostly to generalities and it is comforting to discover that, even in a privileged user environment, the duty not to eat in the library must be specified. It includes a user responsibility which is perhaps most found in informal or semi-formal library environments 'Not to remove stock items from the Library without being formally issued by Library staff'. However, this would not apply in some special library settings which operate on a self-service basis when staff are not on duty. Another is aimed at the problem of non-use which is only beginning to get the recognition it deserves: 'To use our services wherever appropriate to assist with your information needs'. Number 9 is now commonly found in charters and shows clearly the link between evaluation and charters: ' To respond to our requests for feedback whenever possible so that we can evaluate and thus improve our services'.

Service level agreements in higher education libraries

Although not widespread (Revill & Ford 1994) service level agreements in higher education libraries are worth mentioning because they signal a move away from informal promises about levels of library provision to users in favour of explicit guarantees about levels of service which can be subject to evaluation. Service level agreements may be the result of pressure from departments or faculties and they can be seen as a defence mechanism. If questioned or attacked the library can refer to its agreement and point out that it is performing according to it. They can also be used to set limits to demand. It is important to involve library staff who will, after all, be providing the service promised in the agreement, to initiate discussions with users and create a series of partnerships with faculties. The agreement, when it is finally achieved, should have an annual review process which, in turn, supports the overall concept of evaluation. A continuing dialogue should be maintained with users through formal mechanisms like the library committee and informally via faculty meetings.

Leeds Metropolitan University Library has a service level agreement, completed in 1994, which originally began with only one faculty and now applies to all schools and faculties.

The agreement has four aims:

1)   to spell out what the library provides
2)   to set standards of service for the library and mechanisms by which those standards can be monitored
3)   to emphasise the necessity for close co-operation between the library and faculties/schools if the library is to provide a quality service.
4)   to encourage improvements in the range and standards of service provided by the library.

The agreement is intended to evolve as new services are provided. The areas it covers are: assessing user needs, opening hours, study environment, library resources, inter-library-loans, information handling skills, information services and photocopying. Specific topics mentioned include complaints, noise, seat occupancy and shelf tidying.

Clearly service level agreements have an important part to play in providing yardsticks for evaluation and promoting service improvements and, like charters, they need the involvement and support of both library staff and users in their design, implementation and monitoring. However, agreements are not contracts and although service level agreements oblige library services to deliver a certain level of service to users they put no enforceable obligations on users. The library can really only state that it cannot deliver on specifics unless certain user obligations are first met e.g. the library cannot promise to have sufficient copies of a particular textbook available by a particular time unless reading lists are delivered by a mutually agreed date.

Examples of relevant research projects

The following three projects reflect current preoccupations in LIS evaluation research:

Best Value and Better Performance in Libraries: October 1999 - March 2000 (Library and Information Commission funded)

The project explores and evaluates approaches to assessing the impact of public library and schools library services, and develops and tests appropriate models for constructing performance indicators and targets for Public Library Services in the context of 'Best Value'.

The project objectives are to: analyse relevant publications and current initiatives focused on evaluating libraries and library services or other services with comparable features; establish the extent to which public library services are already employ-

ing relevant output and outcome performance indicators and targets and what can be learned from
this experience; review the experience of applying
'Best Value' to assess public library services; consider how 'Best Value' approaches can be developed to ensure high quality evidence to assess the
impact of services (relating 'Best Value' results to
outputs and outcomes in library development
plans); develop and test one or more models for
arriving at reliable and useful output and outcome
performance indicators and targets relevant to
public library service development in a 'Best Value'
context; prepare guidance on how best to use the
model or models in practice; test a particular approach to evaluating research through 'electronic
evaluation panels'.

The emphasis throughout this project will be on
developing models to enable public library service
managers to adopt qualitative performance indicators in a 'Best Value' context. The project will
help managers undertake development actively
based on manageable numbers, with realistic and
achievable key targets reflecting an appropriate
balance of process, output and outcome success
factors.

A Mass Observation of the Contemporary Public Library carried out by Leeds Metropolitan University: June 1999 to 31st March 2000 (Library and Information Commission funded)

The project generated a significant and extensive
'open access' public commentary on public library
activity and status, the purpose of which is to show

where the institution stands in the public eye. Evidence collected points to why public libraries are used, what they do well, what they do badly and, above all, what they mean to users and non-users alike. The data-gathering stage of the research was conducted by the Mass Observation Archive, University of Sussex, an organisation with a long tradition in, and a strong reputation for, conducting sophisticated unobtrusive research into everyday social practices and attitudes. Written observations were obtained from approximately 500 covert volunteers. It was intended that objectivity would be increased by avoiding the interview/survey or observation methodology, where researcher influence tends to sully data and limit its validity. Evidence was largely unprompted, arising from a large number of unprioritised issues and topics presented objectively to volunteers to stimulate commentary. The archive assembled will be made available at the Mass Observation archive, free of charge, to researchers other than the project's proposers. It is anticipated that results of analysis, including those produced by the project team, will benefit public library policy-makers and strategists looking to deepen their understanding of the social context in which public libraries operate.

The EQUINOX Project: Library Performance Measurement and Quality Management System

EQUINOX is a project funded under the Telematics for Libraries Programme of the European Commission. This project addresses the need of all libraries to develop and use methods for measuring performance in the new networked, electronic environment, alongside traditional performance measurement, and to operate these methods within a framework of quality management.

The project has two main objectives. Firstly, EQUINOX aims to further develop existing international agreement on performance measures for libraries, by expanding these to include performance measures for the electronic library environment. The second aim is to develop and test an integrated quality management and performance measurement tool for library managers. The actual details of the Equinox project are discussed in Chapter 6. An interesting feature of the project is its website which is being used as a key method of disseminating information and news about the ongoing work of the project. Feedback is welcome and the website can be visited at http://equinox.dcu.ie/

The specific objectives of the EQUINOX project are:

• To develop an integrated software tool which will assist European librarians to manage increasingly hybrid (i.e. traditional print-based and electronic) libraries in an effective and efficient manner.

• To develop a standard set of performance indicators for the hybrid library and to move towards international agreement on this set.

• To identify the datasets that need to be collected for these performance indicators.

• To provide software which will encourage all library managers to introduce an appropri-

103

ate level of quality management, without the constraints of ISO9000.

- To validate and test the pre-production prototype system in a number of libraries.
- To undertake large scale demonstration trials in libraries across Europe.
- To undertake dissemination of the approach and model across Europe.
- To ensure that Europe retains its world lead in this area.

An example of a fee-based service

The allocation of costs to services has not been looked at in this book but a short study from Telford College in Edinburgh (Glancy 1995) shows how some of these issues can be addressed. It looked at the library's income and expenditure and attempted to apportion income to specific services. Telford College has about 14,000 students and the larger of its two libraries has a stock of some 16,000 items, 106 study places and 2 CD-ROM workstations. The number of registered users is about 25% of total student numbers and this low level of market penetration, common in FE colleges in Scotland, shows the difficulties of the situation. Information was needed in three areas:

1) number of people using the library
2) amount spent on the library
3) income generated in the study period.

The total expenditure for 1994/95 was mainly in the areas of supplies which included books, periodicals, audio-visual and IT costs, postage and telephone calls, staff costs and capital expenditure. Some costs were difficult or impossible to allocate because of insufficient information from the Finance Office. Income also presented problems. Photocopying was the main form of cash income and there were also minor items like sale of computer disks and stationery, fines and sale of withdrawn stock. Some money also came in transfers from other departments and from consultancy services. Enrolment fees were included although the library does not get any money from them. Total cash income, calculated from these sources in 1994/5 was £9,718.76, not far short of the notional target of £10,000 which had been set. A further rise in income is problematical. To achieve further increases from the same number of users it would be necessary to increase charges for more services, whose usage might then decline. External and corporate membership could, however, be increased. The study assumes that increased resources will lead to increased usage, but this in turn, will require increased investment. The study concludes that much more detailed and accurate data is necessary and that the performance indicators used did not measure the *quality* of the services being marketed. Although limited to one library the study shows the difficulties in apportioning costs to services, calculating income accurately and promoting the services to obtain the maximum return.

6. Performance Measurement for the Electronic Library

Definitions

In discussing the electronic library various terms have been used almost interchangeably: the electronic library, the virtual library and the digital library. The term the Hybrid Library is used to denote a mixed collection of traditional paper and electronic sources. At the most basic level a library has been traditionally thought of as a building with carefully selected and pre-determined resources in it. Although the electronic library is not like this it does have some traditional characteristics like being at least partly housed in a building and requiring the support of professional staff although some of these will not be librarians. However, the electronic library entails a movement away from the library as place. The Equinox project defines a library collection as 'All information resources provided by a library for its users. Comprises resources held locally and remote resources for which access has been acquired, at least for a certain period of time'. The definition offered by the Equinox Project (Equinox 1999) of electronic library services is – 'The electronic documents and databases the library decides to make available in its collections, plus the library OPAC and home page'.

What the electronic library does

The electronic library is part of a wider networked environment which offers access to a wide range of materials including internal management information about the host institution and its working environment. It is an organised environment yet paradoxically facilitates extremely anarchic patterns of use. User understanding or lack of it will necessarily influence judgements about its effectiveness. Users may view it as just a collection of computers in a room or as a collection of software packages and networked services which have no essential link with electronic information.

It gives virtual access to book and journal collections and databases. Some of the data contained in these services may be bibliographical control data or metadata, rather than full text. Sources might include bibliographic databases as well as full text sources and paper sources which are, at least, 'virtually' accessed through the OPAC. It augments the traditional materials provided by library services with electronic access to datasets and images such as videoclips which might be used for educational purposes. The service is less building and direct access dependent than the traditional library. The library is the interface to electronic data providing remote access including 24 hour access. Navigational aids and resources are usually provided in the form of 'hotlinked' web pages.

Among the services the electronic library might offer are the following:

• Access to electronic journals

- Word Processing packages
- Excel and other statistical packages
- PowerPoint demonstration software
- Links to local networks
- Internet
- Email
- Bibliographic software
- Digitised books and journals
- Electronic information databases
- OPACs
- Networked CD-ROMs on local area networks
- Full text outputs via bibliographic searching
- Sets of lecture notes
- Web based training packages.

Users and usage

The electronic library redefines the concept of the user and introduces the idea of the 'virtual visitor' or user. The user is no longer someone who 'comes in' and observes set opening hours. There is no defined service period. Users may be accessing the electronic library remotely from home or work and may be seen only infrequently by librarians. Skill levels of users are very variable and may not necessarily be defined by traditional stakeholder groups. It might be necessary to redefine stakeholder groups based on skill levels e.g. older people (Spiller 1998, p. 75) or non-traditional students who conventionally have lower IT skills levels than full-time students. There are likely to be 'regulars' among the user group such as overseas students in higher education or enthusiastic school-children in public libraries. Other types of user include distance and lifelong learners and teleworkers. Conversely there is the problem of non-use which includes such issues as technophobia, and low IT skills among the unemployed and low skill groups. These new characteristics naturally affect the delivery of training as traditional face-to-face-based training can only cope with a fraction of the potential user group and cannot cope at all with remote users. Web-based training, although a powerful tool, can only be used by those with some basic skills.

Identifying performance issues and performance indicators

It is perhaps best to begin by going back to basics and identifying what constitutes a 'good' performance indicator (Harnesk 1998). A good performance indicator should meet the following criteria.

- *Informative content*: should be usable for measuring an activity, for identifying achievements and identifying problems and shortcomings.

- *Reliability*: Produces the same or a similar result if the measurement is repeated.

- *Validity*: measures what it is intended to measure and not something else.

- *Appropriateness*: the operations necessary to implement the process of measurement should fit in with the library's procedures, physical layout etc.

- *Practicality*: the indicator shall use data that can be made available with a reasonable amount of effort and resources.
- *Comparability*: comparing the performance of one library with another is a controversial area. Comparative performance measurement for the electronic library will encounter enormous problems although the potential is equally enormous.

Performance issues

In planning performance indicators for the electronic library issues to be considered include the following:

- Skill levels – In traditional evaluation and performance measurement it is assumed that users do not need high skill levels to comment intelligently on services. Users' comments on services have to be interpreted in the knowledge that IT skill levels vary widely.
- Real use vs. browsing – Is the user making serious, systematic use of a range of electronic services or engaging in unstructured browsing?
- Recreational use – Are services being used for leisure, entertainment or inconsequential purposes? This is an important factor in academic libraries where demand for access to machines is high.
- Provision of unwanted/unanticipated services – The electronic library, because it gives access to the Internet gives access to a range

of information sources which librarians cannot anticipate or control.

- Queuing/booking/walk-outs – Can physical access be easily measured?

- Remote logging in/problems with – Relates to wider issues of network access.

- Problems of outputting data – Printing, downloading to disk and emailing of results. Printing problems include the organisation of printing and whether all computers are linked to a central printer. How is queuing organised and what are the charging mechanisms? Printers usually require at least intermittent staff intervention and staffing support is a quantifiable issue. Floppy disks can involve problems of following proper procedures and may require advice from staff. Damaged disks are another problem.

- No defined service period – Service periods can be intermittent and/or outwith standard opening hours.

- Quality and reliability of Internet data – This is extremely variable and the librarian has no means of exercising any control over it.

- Non-use – This is an extremely complex issue and involves such factors as physical distance from the campus, access to a computer at home or at work, access to a network connection, licensing conditions of databases, IT skill levels, technophobia as well as social class characteristics.

- Changes over time – Longitudinal studies will be affected by changing and hopefully improving skill levels, changes and hopefully improvements in services, changing password authorisations etc.

- Distributed resources – Clusters of computers in different places, perhaps not even in same building make supervision, observation and support difficult.

- Problems outwith the library's control e.g. unreliable networks.

- The service orientated culture – Librarianship is increasingly a service and evaluation-orientated culture but librarians have to work increasingly with IT personnel, not necessarily in a structured environment. If IT personnel mainly concern themselves with technical issues difference in service attitudes can emerge.

- PCs versus Macs – Dual platform services raise training issues for support staff.

The overall picture from these points is that there is a battery of qualitative issues to be considered that count-based methods will fail to recognise and interpret.

Equinox indicators

The Equinox Project is an EU-funded research project which aims to develop international agreement on standard performance measures for the electronic library environment, building on existing agreements for traditional library services.

It proposes the following draft list of performance indicators:

1. Percentage of target population reached by electronic library services.

2. Number of log-ins to electronic library services per capita per month.

3. Number of remote log-ins to electronic library services per capita per month.

4. Number of·electronic documents delivered per capita per month.

5. Cost per log-in per electronic library service.

6. Cost per electronic document delivered per electronic library service.

7. Reference enquiries submitted electronically per capita per month.

8. Library computer workstation use rate.

9. Number of library computer workstations per capita.

10. Library computer workstation hours used per capita per month.

11. Rejected log-ins as a percentage of total log-ins.

12. Systems availability.

13. Mean waiting time for access to library computer workstations.

14. IT expenditure as a percentage of total library expenditure.

This extremely concise list has been refined from an initial list of over fifty indicators which shows how difficult it is to identify reliable performance indicators which can be widely used. They are extremely practical and cover essential areas but should be considered in the light of the largely qualitative issues raised above.

The list does not include length of session which might not, in any case, be very meaningful and there is no real way of measuring success in use and the qualitative level of work undertaken. The proposed performance indicators will be supported by user surveys to gather qualitative information which will complement the numeric nature of the performance indicator set.

The use of electronic services in practice

The mismatch between quantitative indicators and the qualitative issues which need to be addressed shows clearly that programmes of evaluation will continue to be needed but there are surprisingly few studies of this important area. One of the first was undertaken at Munster University. Obst (1995) found that email and the Internet were the services mostly used by students and these mainly for private purposes. A survey of web use by undergraduate business school students at the University of Sunderland (McKeever 1998) was undertaken in May 1997. This showed that most respondents experienced such difficulties in navigating the web that its potential use value was greatly diminished. There was a conspicuous lack of awareness about web information gateways. 'Entertainment purposes' also accounted for a sig-

nificant proportion of web use; 81% of respondents encountered problems frequently or occasionally. Students customarily sought help from other
students. Search engines were not found to be very
helpful.

A study at Glasgow Caledonian University study
confirmed these findings. A mixture of qualitative
methods was used (Crawford 1999) consisting of
47 semi-structured interviews and three independently facilitated focus groups. The questionnaire
method was not used because of a lack of clearly
defined performance issues on which to base questionnaire questions.

Some conclusions from the study were as follows:

*   The distinctive mission of the Library's Elec-
    tronic Information Floor (EIF) was not clear
    to users who simply viewed it as a collection
    of computers located in the Library.
*   Much of the use was unsophisticated and
    centred on email, the Internet and word
    processing. Electronic information services
    were less used.
*   There was a good deal of non-curricular use
    centring around using email and the Internet
    for recreational purposes.
*   Levels of IT skills were low especially among
    non-traditional students.
*   Much of the learning was from other students
    and not from Library or other staff.

The study also highlighted general issues requiring
further study. Users did not appear to distinguish
between electronic services generally like email and

word processing packages and specific electronic information services like Science Citation Index. They saw the matter more in terms of 'things you can do on a computer'. A follow-up study undertaken in Spring 1999 showed that only about 15% of computer user was devoted to the use of electronic information services.

These findings have been confirmed by an elaborate study at Cornell University (Payette & Rieger 1998) which used a combination of different techniques such as observation, semi structured interviews, a questionnaire and focus groups. This found a wide ignorance of the electronic sources available and how they are accessed. Staff typically only used two or three databases and none of the students used the library-provided web gateway to access databases although they did use internet search engines to locate information for course work. Staff and students both wanted swift access to relevant material with minimal investment in learning and searching time. The overall picture is of unsophisticated use. Whether this will change over time is one the biggest issues in evaluation of the electronic library.

Survey methods

There is clearly a major evaluation challenge here. McClure & Lopata's (1996) pioneering work is concerned with assessing University campus networks rather than the evaluation of electronic information services but the repertoire of techniques they recommend is relevant and surprisingly traditional. Because evaluating the academic networking environment is in its early stages qualitative techniques will be especially useful in developing an understanding of the users of networks as well as the benefits and problems associated with network use. Participants can raise issues which the evaluator did not anticipate. The range of qualitative methods prescribed includes focus groups, user activity logs (diaries), interviews and observational methods. For effective observation a well-developed data collection form is essential. Quantitative methods (questionnaires) can also be used.

The following methodologies can all be used: software-based counts, observation, one-to-one interviews, focus groups, diaries and questionnaires, both offline and online. There are, however, particular problems with evaluation of the electronic library. Observational techniques work well provided a data sheet is used so that the observer can work systematically. Observation, however, requires considerable IT expertise as the observer must be able to recognise what service is being used and form some impressions of the user's IT skills. Observation also tends to be unsuited to the study of remote users. Questionnaires can be administered either on paper or electronically. Paper-based questionnaires require no IT expertise to complete and consequently produce a less biased return but response rates tend to be low. Electronic questionnaires, made available over OPACs, have been experimented with (Webster 1995) although the method has disadvantages. In this case completion rates were less than 10%. Experience of administering questionnaires electronically at Glasgow Caledonian University, on the other hand, shows that response rates are high but, as rudimentary IT skills are required to complete them, the sample is necessarily biased. While the use of a range of techniques facilitates comparisons (triangulation) and consequently validates the data, systematic evaluation of the electronic library may prove to be extremely labour-intensive because of the range of skills needed and the importance of human-based qualitative studies. All this assumes that the use of electronic services is rich and varied and worthy of serious investigation. If future survey work shows this not to be the case then the problem will be smaller.

Outcomes and consequences

Equinox draft indicators 5, 6 and 14:

> '5. cost per log-in per electronic library service
>
> 6. cost per electronic document delivered per electronic library service
>
> 14. IT expenditure as a percentage of total library expenditure'

suggest that performance measurement for the electronic library will be much more of an overtly accounting exercise than previous forms of evaluation or performance measurement. It should be possible to look at usage of specific services and decide whether the money spent on them is justified. It will be easier to identify demand in general and demand in particular subject areas. It should help libraries to assess what to do with the money they have and correlate funding more precisely with users' needs. While, in the short term, the number of electronic databases libraries subscribe to is likely to increase, in the long run, measurement of use might lead to stabilisation and indeed reduction if some databases are found to be little used. Already English language information databases predominate and standardised methods of measurement might hasten this process, except perhaps in the area of social sciences where there seems to be a continuing demand for databases of publications presented in languages other than English. There may also be implications for information-seeking skills training, for if it becomes possible to identify a limited number of widely used electronic information databases, then it might be possible to devise a training programme, based round them, rather in the manner of the European Computer Driving Licence, setting out a programme of basic training in IT skills. Overall, however, the changing behaviour of users may be the biggest issue especially if the UK government's lifelong learning initiative generates a demand for electronic information among people previously unfamiliar with such sources. This will be a challenge for both public and educational libraries.

The future

The past few years has seen the spread of the performance indicator movement and the prescription of reliable tested performance indicators together with methodologies for their application. It remains to be seen whether this will inhibit the evaluation movement with the wide range of methodologies at its disposal. The application of the Best Value regime in public libraries may lead to the appointment of quality officers but wider progress to such a movement will be dependent on the application of standardised quality programmes which would themselves be necessary to promote the regular collection of a wide range of performance indicators.

While public libraries progress a key set of performance indicators the picture in higher education is still emerging. The Cranfield project recommended a set of nine key 'management statistics' to be used by British academic libraries (Barton 1998) and a first set covering the university and larger higher education college libraries was published in 1999 (SCONUL & HCLRG 1999). SCONUL and HCLRG intend to maintain the series in future years if possible.

Evaluation will certainly be needed to understand the new challenges of electronic information and lifelong and distance learning, a world in which contact with the user will be irregular and perhaps infrequent. Evaluation will be needed to support the development of charters and expectation management for here the move to a customer-based model, disability rights legislation and the possibilities offered by the electronic information revolution will all need to be considered.

As services other than libraries within an organisation develop their own programmes of evaluation the evaluation of library and information services may decline as a separate issue although the standards set by librarians will surely continue to be influential. In higher education evaluation is increasingly seen as a holistic exercise in which the students' experience is evaluated as a whole rather than just one aspect of it. Performance issues can emerge from this process which are common to several departments, rather than just the library. Communication is a very good example (Crawford 2000).

Another factor, which is receiving increasing attention, is the influence of outside forces. It is no longer possible to think of library users as people who have no measurable life other than as library users. In higher education the increasing need for students to have employment lessens their contact with university services and requires more flexible modes of provision. Services must be planned and evaluated with this in mind. In public libraries LISU and the South East London Performance Indicator Group (SELPIG) have studied the relationship between social deprivation in a local authority area and library use. This showed that there is a statistical relationship between deprivation and library performance and has led to further work (Creaser 1998). So the future may be both more 'holistic' and more sociological in character.

7. Further reading

Abbott, C. Performance indicators in a quality context, *Law librarian,* 25 (4), 1994, pp. 205-208

Abbott, C. *Performance measurement in library and information services,* London, Aslib. 1994.

Alston, R. Performance indicators in Bromley: purpose and practice, *Library management,* 16 (1), 1995. pp.18-28

Audit Commission. *Due for renewal: a report on the library service,* London, Audit Commission, 1997

Barton, J. The recommendations of the Cranfield project on performance indicators for academic libraries, *SCONUL Newsletter,* 14 Autumn, 1998, pp. 15-17

Barton, J and Blagden, J. *Academic library effectiveness: a comparative approach,* London, British Library Research and Innovation Centre, 1998 (British Library Research and Innovation Report 120)

Batchelor, K and Tyerman, K. Expressions of interest in Brent, *Library Association Record,* 96 (10), 1994, pp. 554-555

Bawden, D. *User-orientated evaluation of information systems and services,* Aldershot, Gower, 1990

Blagden, J and Harrington, J. *How good is your library? : a review of approaches to the evaluation of library and information services,* London, Aslib, 1990

Bohme, S. and Spiller, D. *Perspectives of public library use 2 : a compendium of survey information*, Loughborough, LISU, 1999

British Standards Institution. *Information and documentation: library performance indicators*, London, BSI, 1998 (International Standard ISO 11620)

Brophy, P. and Coulling, K. *Quality management for information and library managers*, London, Aslib, 1996

Buch, H. Benutzerzufriedenheitsstudie 1996 der Universitats-und Landesbibliothek, Munster oder "...hier scheint mir alles wunderbar und perfekt!", *Bibliokteksdienst* 31, (1) 1997, pp. 23-31

Cabinet Office. *How to apply for a Charter Mark 1999: a guide for applicants*, London, Cabinet Office, 1998

CIPFA. *Public library statistics 1998/99 actuals*, London, CIPFA, 1999

Clarke, Z., McDougall, A. and Fisher, S. An opportunity for software development in library quality management and performance measurement: the EQLIPSE experience. *Proceedings of the 2nd Northumbria international conference on performance measurement in libraries and information services.* Newcastle, Information North, 1998, pp. 405-412

Committee of Vice-Chancellors and Principals of the Universities of the United Kingdom. Universities Staff Development Unit. *Student feedback – context, issues and practice*, ed. by P. Partington, Sheffield, CVCP / USDU, 1993

Crawford, J. C. The stakeholder approach to the construction of performance measures *Proceedings of the 1st Northumbria international conference on performance measurement in libraries and information services,* Newcastle, Information North, 1995, pp. 177-185

Crawford, J. C. A qualitative study of the use of networked software and electronic information services at Glasgow Caledonian University Library, *Education for information,* 17, (2), 1999, pp.101-111

Crawford, J. C.'"It's LIS evaluation, Jim, but not as we know it": the implications of the ESEP Project', in *Proceedings of the 3rd Northumbria International Conference on Performance Measurement in Library and Information Services,* Newcastle upon Tyne, Information North, 2000, pp. 75-80

Creaser, C. *Modelling use at individual service points,* Loughborough, LISU, 1998 (LISU Occasional Paper no. 18)

Creaser, C. and Murphy, A. *A survey of library services to schools and children in the UK 1998 –99,* Loughborough, LISU, 1999

Creaser, C. and Murphy, A. *LISU annual library statistics 1999: featuring trend analysis of UK public and academic libraries 1988-98. Including Public Library Statistics Report No. 13,* Loughborough, LISU, 1999

Creaser, C, and Spiller, D. *TFPL survey of UK special library statistics,* Loughborough, LISU, 1997 (LISU Occasional Paper no. 15)

Crist, M., Daub, P. and MacAdam, B. User studies: reality check and future perfect, *Wilson Library Bulletin*, 68 (6), 1994, pp. 38-41

Cullen, R. J. and Calvert, P. J. Stakeholder perceptions of university library effectiveness, *Journal of academic librarianship* Nov, 1995, pp. 438-448

Department of National Heritage. *Reading the future: a review of public libraries in England*, London, Department for Culture, Media and Sport, 1997

East Renfrewshire Council. *Library survey 1999: summary of results*, 1999, unpublished

England, L & Sumsion, J. *Perspectives of public library use: a compendium of survey information*, Loughborough, LISU, 1995

Equinox. *Library Performance Measurement and Quality Management System.* [online] Equinox, 1999. Available from http://equinox.dcu.ie/index.html [Accessed Dec. 1999]

Everhart, N. *Evaluating the school library media center: analysis techniques and research practices*, Englewood, Libraries Unlimited, 1998

Forrest, M. and Mackay, D. A healthy relationship with your user, *Library Association Record*, 101 (8), 1999, p. 476

Glancy, M. Edinburgh's Telford College: costs per registered user and income generated as a percentage of costs, *Improving libraries: case studies on implementing performance indicators in Scottish college libraries*, Glasgow, Scottish Further Education Unit, 1995, pp. 53-67

Goodall, D. Use of diaries in library and information research, *Library and information research news*, 18 (59), 1994, pp. 17-21

Gorman, G E & Clayton, P. *Qualitative research for the information professional*, London, Library Association Publishing, 1997

Harnesk, J. The ISO standard on library performance indicators (ISO 11620), *Proceedings of the 2nd Northumbria international conference on performance measurement in libraries and information services.* Newcastle, Information North, 1998, pp. 61-65

Hart, E. The role of focus groups with other performance measurement methods, *Proceedings of the 1st Northumbria international conference on performance measurement in libraries and information services.* Newcastle, Information North, 1995, pp. 277-282

HEFC Colleges Learning Resources Group. *Statistics 1997/98*, HCLRG, 1999 (Available from David Brown, Harold Bridges Library, St Martin's College, Lancaster)

Improving libraries: case studies on implementing performance indicators in Scottish college libraries, Glasgow, Scottish Further Education Unit, 1995

IPF. *A standard for the undertaking of user surveys in public libraries in the United Kingdom: manual of guidance*, London, CIPFA, 1995

Joint Funding Councils. *The effective academic library: a framework for evaluating the performance of UK academic libraries*, Bristol, Higher Education Funding Council for England, 1995

Joint Funding Councils' Libraries Review Group. *Report*, Bristol, Higher Education Funding Council for England (Follett Report), 1993

King Research Ltd. *Keys to success: performance indicators for public libraries*, (Library Information series no. 18). London, Office of Arts and Libraries, 1990

Krejcie, R. V. and Morgan, D W. Determining sample size for research activity. *Educational and psychological measurement*, 30, 1970, pp. 607-610

Lancaster, F. W. *If you want to evaluate your library*, 2nd ed., London, Library Association, 1993

Library Association. *The Charter approach*, London: Library Association Publishing, 1992

Library Association. *A charter for public libraries*, London, Library Association Publishing, 1993

Library Association. *Model statement of standards*, London, Library Association Publishing, 1995

Library Association. Survey *of UK secondary school libraries 1997*, London, Library Association, 1997

Library Association. Branch and Mobile Libraries Group. *Charter for public mobile library services*, London, Library Association, 1997

Library Association. Colleges of Further and Higher Education Group. *Guidelines for college libraries: recommendations for performance and resourcing*, 5th ed. London, Library Association Publishing, 1995

Line M. B. and Stone, S. *Library surveys: an introduction to the use, planning, procedure and presentation of surveys*, London, Clive Bingley, 1982

McClure, C. R. and Lopata C L. *Assessing the academic networked environment: strategies and options*, Washington, Coalition for Networked Information, 1996

McKeever, L. *Intellectual resource or digital haystack? web experiences of undergraduate business school students*, [online] IRISS '98 Conference papers. SOSIG, 1998. Available from: http://www.sosig.ac.uk/iriss/papers/paper20.htm [Accessed August 1998]

Mendelsohn, S. Does your library come up to scratch? *Library manager*, 8, June, 1995, pp. 6-9

Ministry of Defence. HQ Information and Library Service. *Library service charter*, MOD, 1998

Morgan, S. *Performance assessment in academic libraries*, London, Mansell, 1995

Obst, O. *Untersuchung der Internetbenutzung durch Bibliothekskunden an der Universitaets-und Landesbibliothek (ULB) Muenster*, Bibliotheksdienst, 29, 12, 1995 , pp. 1980-1998

Open Polytechnic of New Zealand. *Student library service*, Lower Hutt, Open Polytechnic of New Zealand, 1998

Payette, S. D. and Rieger, O. Y. Supporting scholarly inquiry: incorporating users in the design of the digital library, *Journal of academic librarianship*, March, 1998, pp. 121-129

Poll, R. and te Boekhorst, P. *Measuring quality: international guidelines for performance measurement in academic libraries*, Munchen, Saur, 1996 (IFLA Publications 76)

Pritchard, T. A plus for Leeds, *Library Association Record,* 97 (10), 1995, pp. 549-550

Public Libraries, *Which* February 1990, pp108-110

Revill, D H. Adapting US academic library standard survey forms for use in UK libraries, *Proceedings of the 1st Northumbria international conference on performance measurement in libraries and information services.* Newcastle, Information North, 1995 pp. 115-125

Revill, D. H. and Ford, G., eds. *Working papers on service level agreements,* London, SCONUL, 1994

Review of the public library service in England and Wales for the Department of National Heritage: final report, London, Aslib, 1995

SCONUL. *User satisfaction: standard survey forms for academic libraries,* London, SCONUL, 1996 (SCONUL briefing paper)

SCONUL. *Aide-memoire for assessors when evaluating library and computing services,* London, SCONUL, 1997 Available at http://www.sconul.ac.uk/aidememoire.html

SCONUL. *Annual library statistics 1997-98.* London, SCONUL, 1999

SCONUL and HCLRG. *UK higher education library management statistics 1997-98,* London, SCONUL & HCLRG, 1999

Scottish Higher Education Funding Council. *Quality assessment annual report 1997-1998,* Edinburgh, SHEFC, 1998

Scottish Library and Information Council & Scottish Library Association. *Libraries in Scottish further education colleges: standards for performance and resourcing,* Motherwell, Scottish Library & Information Council, 1997

Slater, M., ed. *Research methods in library and information studies,* London, Library Association Publishing, 1990

Spiller, D., ed. *Public library plans: proceedings of seminar held at Loughborough University,* Loughborough, LISU, 1998 (LISU Occasional Paper no. 19)

Spiller, D., Creaser, C. and Murphy, A. *Libraries in the workplace,* Loughborough, LISU, 1998 (LISU Occasional Paper no. 20)

Spreadbury, H & Spiller, D. *Survey of secondary school library users,* Loughborough, LISU, 1999 (LISU Occasional Paper no. 21).

Stephen, P & Hornby, S. *Simple statistics for library and information professionals*, London, Library Association Publishing, 1995

Sumsion, J. *Practical performance indicators - 1992. Documenting the Citizens' Charter consultation for UK public libraries with examples of PIs and surveys in use, (Occasional Paper no. 5).* Loughborough, LISU, 1993

Sumsion, J. *Survey of resources & uses in higher education libraries: UK 1993, (Occasional paper no. 6.)* Loughborough, LISU, 1994

Town J S. Benchmarking and performance measurement, *Proceedings of the 1st Northumbria international conference on performance measurement in libraries and information services*. Newcastle, Information North, 1995, pp. 83-88

University of Central England in Birmingham. Centre for Research into Quality. *The 1998 report on the student experience at UCE*, Birmingham, University of Central England, 1998

University of London. *Library*. *Customer charter*, London, University of London Library, 1994

Usherwood, B. Quality management and public library services, *Proceedings of the 1st Northumbria international conference on performance measurement in libraries and information services*, Newcastle, Information North, 1995, pp. 269-276

Van House, N. Organisation politics and performance measurement, *Proceedings of the 1st Northumbria international conference on performance measurement in libraries and information services*, Newcastle, Information North, 1995, pp. 1-10

Van House, N, Weil, B T & McClure, C R. *Measuring academic library performance: a practical approach*, Chicago, American Library Association, 1990

Webb, S P. *Making a charge for library and information services*, London, Aslib, 1994

Webb, S P. *Pursuing quality in special libraries: a study of current activities and developments in the United Kingdom, (British Library R & D Report 6214)*. London, British Library Research and Development Department, 1995

Webster, K G. The use of IT in library evaluation: electronic surveying at the University of Newcastle, *Proceedings of the 1st Northumbria international conference on performance measurement in libraries and information services*, Newcastle, Information North, 1995, pp. 193-198

Widdows, R, Hensler, T. A. & Wyncott, M. H. The focus group interview: a method for assessing users' evaluation of library service, *College and research libraries*, 52 (4) 1991, pp. 352-359

Willoughby, C. Library services review at the University of Northumbria, *SCONUL Newsletter*, 17, 1999. pp.33-37.

Wisdom, J. Getting and using student feedback, In: Brew, Angela, ed. *Directions in staff development*, Buckingham, Open University Press, 1995, pp. 81-94

Young, V. Focus on focus groups. *College and research libraries news*, 54 (7), 1993, pp. 391-394

8. List of organisations

Book Marketing Ltd. (BML)

7a Bedford Square
London WC1B 3RA
Tel: 020 7580 7282
http://users.londonweb.net/bookmark/
page1.htm

CERLIM (Centre for Research in Library and Information Management)

Department of Information and Communications
Manchester Metropolitan University
Geoffrey Manton Building
Rosamond Street West
Off Oxford Road
Manchester
M15 6LL
Tel: 0161 247 6142
http://www.mmu.ac.uk/h-ss/cerlim/

CIPFA (Chartered Institute of Public Finance and Accountancy)

3 Robert Street
London WC2N 6BH
Tel: 020 7895 8823

HEFC Colleges Learning Resources Group

Contact: Dr Angela Conyers,
Director of Library Services,
Canterbury Christ Church University College,
North Holmes Road,
Canterbury, Kent,
CT1 1QU
email a.d.conyers@cant.ac.uk

IPF Limited (Institute of Public Finance Limited: the commercial arm of CIPFA)

Suffolk House
College Road
Croydon CRO 1PF
Tel: 0186-667-1144

Library Association

7 Ridgmount Street
London WC1E 7AE
Tel: 020 7255 0500
http://www.la-hq.org.uk/index.html

LISU (The Library & Information Statistics Unit)

Loughborough University
Loughborough
Leics. LE11 3TU
Tel: 01509 223071
http://www-server.lboro.ac.uk/departments/
dils/lisu/about.html

MORI (Market & Opinion Research International)

32 Old Queen Street
London SW1H 9HP
020 7222 0232
http://www.mori.com/

Standing Conference of National and University Libraries (SCONUL)

102 Euston Street
London NW1 2HA
Tel: 020 7387 0317
http://www.sconul.ac.uk/about.htm

Aslib Know How Guides

Assessing Information Needs: Tools, Techniques and Concepts for the Internet Age (2nd ed)

Copyright for Library and Information Service Professionals (2nd ed)

Developing a Records Management Programme

Disaster Planning for Library and Information Services

Effective Financial Planning for Library and Information Services

Email for Library and Information Professionals (2nd ed)

Evaluation of Library and Information Services (2nd ed)

How to Market Your Library Service Effectively (2nd ed)

How to Promote Your Web Site Effectively

Information Resources Selection

The Internet for Library and Information Service Professionals (3rd ed)

Intranets and Push Technology: Creating an Information-Sharing Environment

Job Descriptions for the Information Profession

Knowledge Management: Linchpin of Change

Legal Information – What It Is and Where to Find It (2nd ed)

Legal Liability for Information Provision

Making a Charge for Library and Information Services

Managing Change in Libraries and Information Services

Managing Film and Video Collections

Managing Library Automation

Moving Your Library

Performance Measurement in Library and Information Services

Preparing a Guide to Your Library and Information Service

Project Management for Library and Information Service Professionals

Researching for Business: Avoiding the 'Nice to Know' Trap

Strategic Planning for Library and Information Services

Teleworking for Library and Information Professionals

World Wide Web: How to Design and Construct Web Pages (2nd ed)